SpringerBriefs in Computer Science

Series Editors
Stan Zdonik
Peng Ning
Shashi Shekhar
Jonathan Katz
Xindong Wu
Lakhmi C. Jain
David Padua
Xuemin Shen
Borko Furht

For further volumes:
http://www.springer.com/series/10028

Cameron Browne

Evolutionary Game Design

 Springer

Cameron Browne
Imperial College London
180 Queens Gate
South Kensington London
SW7 2RH
UK
e-mail: camb@doc.ic.ac.uk

ISSN 2191-5768   e-ISSN 2191-5776
ISBN 978-1-4471-2178-7   e-ISBN 978-1-4471-2179-4
DOI 10.1007/978-1-4471-2179-4
Springer London Dordrecht Heidelberg New York

British Library Cataloguing in Publication Data
A catalogue record for this book is available from the British Library

Cover design: eStudio Calamar, Berlin/Figueres

Printed on acid-free paper

Springer is part of Springer Science+Business Media (www.springer.com)

Dedicated to Joan Bolitho for the many games over the years

Preface

This book tells the story of Yavalath, the first computer-generated board game to be commercially released. Much of the material is based on my PhD thesis and subsequent journal article on evolutionary game design, which describe the development of a software system called Ludi that can play, measure and create a range of new board games. Ludi proved successful in automatically generating games that human players find interesting, but its operation also revealed some possible shortcomings of the evolutionary process for game design. The Ludi project is now placed in the broader context of computational creativity, and questions raised by the creation of Yavalath and its subsequent impact since release are examined in detail.

Contents

Chapter 1
Introduction

*Human beings are never more ingenious than in the invention
of games.*

Leibniz

Abstract Yavalath is a recently invented board game which has proven to be
popular with players but is distinguished by one remarkable fact: it is the first
computer-designed board game to be commercially released. This chapter introduces Yavalath and outlines some of the questions that it raises with respect to
computational creativity. Was the invention of Yavalath a creative act? Should the
mantle of creator lie with the programme or the programmer? A brief outline of the
history and motivation behind the Ludi project for evolutionary game design is
presented.

Keywords Computational creativity · Artificial intelligence · Evolutionary game
design · Yavalath · Ludi

1.1 Creativity at Play

In November 2007, a new board game called Yavalath was invented. The rules of
Yavalath are simple: players win by making 4-in-a-row of their colour but lose by
making 3-in-a-row beforehand.

Figure 1.1 shows a Yavalath puzzle by way of example. What is White's only
winning play? Hint: consider what happens if Black is allowed to play at either cell
marked X. The solution can be found in Chap. 7, along with the complete rules and
a more thorough analysis of the game.

Yavalath has proven reasonably popular as its simple rules allow interesting and
surprising situations to develop due to its innovative "win with 4 but lose with 3"
winning condition. It has since gone on to be commercially published, but is set apart
from the many other board games invented in 2007 by one remarkable fact: Yavalath
was designed by a computer programme.

C. Browne, *Evolutionary Game Design*, SpringerBriefs in Computer Science,
DOI: 10.1007/978-1-4471-2179-4_1, © Cameron Browne 2011

Fig. 1.1 Yavalath puzzle:
White to play and win

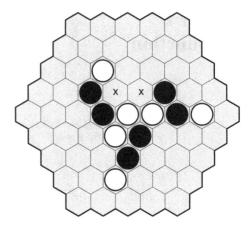

1.1.1 Computational Creativity

The genesis of Yavalath raises an interesting question familiar to many AI prac-
titioners: did the computer invent the game or merely discover it? In other words,
should the mantle of *creator* rest with the programme or the programmer.

This question falls within the realm of *computational creativity*, which explores
whether computer programmes are capable of genuinely creative activity [47].
Combinatorial creativity, a subgenre of this field involving the generation of
artefacts through the combination of elements found in known *inspiring examples*,
is of particular relevance to the creation of Yavalath.

There are three aspects of an artefact that indicate whether creativity has
occurred in its invention:

- *Novelty*: The extent to which it differs from other examples of its genre.
- *Quality*: The quality of the artefact compared to existing examples.
- *Typicality*: The extent to which the artefact belongs to its intended genre.

Boden [9] suggests that a high rating of creativity can also be assigned to the
production of artefacts that are atypical of their genre but which nevertheless rate
highly when judged on their merits. In other words, the genre boundary should not
be a barrier to creativity. In practical terms, a system might therefore be seen as
creative if it can produce artefacts that are novel and of high quality, whether they
are typical of their genre or not.

The extent to which the system *reinvents* known examples is also evidence of
creativity [47]. In Boden's [9] terms, such examples would indicate P-*Creativity*
(psychological creativity novel to the individual) while completely new examples
never seen before would indicate H-*Creativity* (historical creativity). Other indicators of creativity include the extent to which generated artefacts are accepted
among human users or judges, and whether they go on to inspire further creativity
in others.

Fig. 1.2 Creativity in games

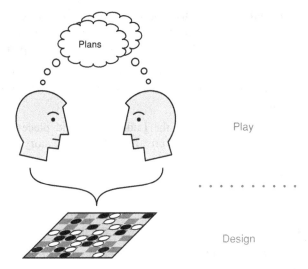

1.1.2 Creativity in Games

Turning now to the domain at hand, the invention of games, Fig. 1.2 shows two aspects of creativity in board games:

1. *Creativity in play* concerns the plans that players develop and the puzzles that they present to each other over the course of a game. Creativity is required to devise new strategies and set unexpected traps for the opponent, and creativity is required by the opponent to detect these strategies and avoid those traps.
2. *Creativity in design*, on the other hand, concerns finding the optimal combination of rules and equipment that allow the most enjoyable contests for the players. Creativity in play is what keeps the game interesting for players, and creativity in design is what allows such interesting games to take place.

There are of course other creative aspects to games including their visual and tactile design, for example in the colour, shape and texture of the board and pieces. However, we are concerned instead with abstract notions of rule quality and how well a game works to provide an engaging contest for the players, rather than how the equipment looks or feels.

The question of computational creativity provides an underlying theme throughout this book. Evidence for creativity in the automated design of games is presented, then summarised in the Conclusion.

1.2 Overview

A recent survey of connection games [13] revealed that many games of this type were essentially mixtures of the same rules in different combinations and contexts, some of which worked well to produce new playing experiences and some of which did not. This observation led to a PhD thesis on combinatorial game design [14], for which a general game framework called Ludi was developed and experiments conducted to explore the following hypotheses:

1. That there exist fundamental (and measurable) indicators of game quality.
2. That these fundamental indicators may be harnessed for the directed search for new high quality games.

This book describes the Ludi system and places these earlier results in the context of computational creativity. It tells the story of Yavalath and other games produced by the system: how they were created, how well they work, and the repercussions since their release. Some new questions regarding the creative process arise:

- Can Ludi's generation of games be deemed 'creative'?
- If so, does the creativity lie with the programme or the programmer?

Games have been studied as a test bed for artificial intelligence (AI) research almost since its inception. They have typically been approached as problems to be solved, and research to date has focussed on the quality of the artificial player. However, some of this research focus is now shifting towards the quality of the games themselves, as they become increasingly popular and procedurally generated content becomes more prevalent. As Pell [43] states:

> If we could develop a program which, upon consideration of a particular game, declared the game to be uninteresting, this would seem to be a true sign of intelligence! So when this becomes an issue, we will know that the field has certainly matured.

1.2.1 Structure

This book is structured as follows:

- Chapter 2 defines the games to be investigated, the elements that make them up, and the issues involved in recombining them into new games.
- Chapter 3 describes the Ludi system, including its game description language and general game player.
- Chapter 4 covers how Ludi measures games for quality through self-play.
- Chapter 5 describes how Ludi evolves new games from known rule sets.
- Chapter 6 describes the 19 viable games produced by Ludi.
- Chapter 7 describes Yavalath in detail.
- Chapter 8 provides a retrospective of the project, where it succeeded and failed, and its implications for computational creativity.

Chapter 2
Games in General

> *You've spent all your life learning games; there can't be a rule,*
> *move, concept or idea... that you haven't encountered ten*
> *times before.*
>
> Iain M. Banks, *Player of Games*

Abstract Combinatorial games make an ideal test bed for the Ludi project as they typically involve simple, well-defined rule sets but complex play. A simple *means-play-ends* model of game play is presented, then combinatorial games and the elements or *ludemes* that make them up are described in this context. While it is simple to recombine the elements of a game into novel configurations that define new games, it is much more difficult to identify those that actually produce a good result. This chapter describes some of the factors involved and how to distinguish new games from mere variants.

Keywords Combinatorial game · Ludeme · Game design · Recombination game · Game variant · Game distance

2.1 Defining Games

Of the many ways to define a game, Salen and Zimmerman [51] make the following useful observation:

> A game is a system in which players engage in an artificial conflict, defined by rules, that results in a quantifiable outcome (p 81).

This definition was condensed from the findings of many prior studies, most of which identified rules, play and outcome as the key elements of a game.

This suggests the basic game model shown in Fig. 2.1, which consists of:

- *Means*: The equipment and rules for playing the game.
- *Play*: The interaction between the players, defined implicitly by the plans they devise and explicitly by the moves they make.
- *Ends*: The resulting outcomes that these moves produce.

C. Browne, *Evolutionary Game Design*, SpringerBriefs in Computer Science,
DOI: 10.1007/978-1-4471-2179-4_2, © Cameron Browne 2011

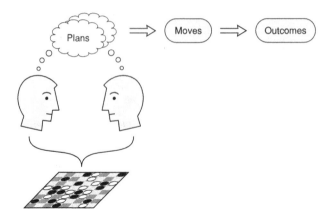

Fig. 2.1 Basic game model

We will follow this basic means-play-ends model at all levels of this study, from the specification of games to their measurement and ultimate creation.

2.1.1 Combinatorial Games

We focus on combinatorial games, which are:

- *Finite*: Produce well-defined outcomes.
- *Discrete*: Turn based.
- *Deterministic*: Chance plays no part.
- *Perfect information*: No hidden information.
- *Two-player*.

Such games may be called abstract games, board games, abstract board games, strategy games or simply abstracts by various players. However, these terms can have different implications for different players depending on their background, so the more precise term combinatorial game is preferred.

The two-player requirement is debatable as solitaire puzzles may validly constitute combinatorial games, in the sense that the puzzle solver competes against the null player and indirectly the designer who set the challenge. Multiplayer games with three or more players fall outside the scope of combinatorial play due to the social aspect of coalitions that may arise.

The term game shall henceforth refer to a two-player combinatorial game throughout this book. Such games are an ideal test bed for the experiments as they are typically deep but described by simple, well-defined rule sets.

Note that this book is not a work in combinatorial game theory (CGT), which is concerned with the analysis of games with a view to solving them or at least finding optimal strategies [7]. For the purposes of this study, the artificial player does not

Fig. 2.2 Games of Tic Tac
Toe and Tic Tac Toe (3D)
won by White

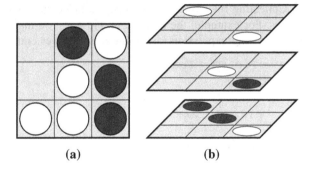

(a)   (b)

need to challenge human experts and is of little interest except as a means for
providing self-play simulations. While the AI must be of sufficient strength to provide meaningful playouts, we are concerned primarily with the quality of the game
itself rather than the quality of the artificial player.

2.2 Game Elements

The following sections show how the rule sets of games can be broken down into
their constituent elements and recombined to create new games. Creating new
games is easy, but creating new high quality games is a much more difficult task.

2.2.1 Ludemes

Just as a meme is a unit of information that replicates from one person to another
[19], a *ludeme* is a game meme or unit of game information. First coined by Borvo
[11], this term describes a fundamental unit of play often equivalent to a rule;
ludemes are the conceptual equivalent of a game's components—both material and
non-material—and are notable for their ability to pass from one game or game
class to another [42].

Ludemes may be single units of information, such as the following items that
describe aspects of the game board shown in Fig. 2.2a:

(*tiling square*)
(*size 3 3*)

Conceptually related items may be encapsulated to form higher level compound
ludemes as follows:

(*board*
  (*tiling square*)
  (*size 3 3*)

)

Collecting rules into such compound ludemes is a convenient way to describe games. For example, the essence of Tic Tac Toe may be succinctly described in the following expression (assuming a two-player combinatorial model):

```
(game Tic-Tac-Toe
   (board
      (tiling square)
      (size 3 3)
   )
   (win (in-a-row 3))
)
```

The concept of an entire game as a single item of information may seem odd but it is valid; there exist many examples of identical games being discovered, fully formed, at similar times. The most famous case is the independent discovery of Hex by mathematicians Piet Hein and John Nash in the 1940s [12]. A more recent example is Chameleon, discovered by New Zealand and USA designers within a week of each other in 2003. Such cases may be examples of "memetic convergence" in action towards optimal designs. Combinatorial games are typically described by simple, well-defined rules, making them especially amenable to such encapsulation.

2.2.2 Variants

Given a game in its ludemic form, it is a simple matter to manipulate its rules to create variants and new games. For Tic Tac Toe, such modifications might include the board size:

```
(size 2 2)
```

or the target line length:

```
(win (in-a-row 2))
```

However, a moment's reflection will reveal that each of these changes break the game, by making it unwinnable in the first case and trivially winnable in the second. Other manipulations might involve extending the board to three dimensions, as shown in Fig. 2.2b:

```
(size 3 3 3)
```

or inverting the end condition to give a misere version:

```
(lose (in-a-row 3))
```

These variants are both more interesting but still trivially solvable, and are more notable for their novelty value than any inherent value as games. There is much room for improvement in this branch of the N–in-a-row family.

2.2.3 Recombination Games

The difficulty of deriving an interesting game from Tic Tac Toe does not just stem from the fact that it is itself flawed (it is drawish if played correctly). There is the serious problem that rule sets for combinatorial games tend to be highly optimised and fragile; authors strive for the simplest rule sets that give the deepest playing experience, and the slightest change to a rule set will generally break the game. As with most creative tasks, it is easy to generate artificial content but much more difficult to generate artificial content of human expert quality.

It is unlikely that simple manipulations of an optimised rule set will produce an even better game in isolation, as the designer would usually have tested such obvious variants and discarded them as inferior. A more promising approach is to recombine the game's rules with rules from other games and look for the emergence [27] of interesting, new rule combinations not previously considered.

The rule sets of good games represent local maxima in the game design landscape, and any small changes to those rules will only go downhill in most cases. True innovation will occur when large changes move the search to another part of the design landscape where iterative improvement can climb a different local maxima, hopefully one that has not been explored before.

The idea that there pre-exist a multitude of games in the form of optimal rule combinations waiting to be discovered resonates strongly with the Platonist view of mathematics [28]. The question then becomes how to search this potentially huge design space effectively, and what fitness measure to use to guide the search. This task is an exercise in combinatorial creativity, and it is fortuitous that combinatorial games are not only combinatorial in play, but also combinatorial in design.

2.2.4 Game Distance

It can be useful to measure the distance of a newly devised rule set from known games to determine whether it constitutes a:

- duplicate,
- variant, or
- completely new game.

The distinction between a variant and a new game is subtle, but may be achieved by representing both games as rule trees and performing standard tree comparison to find the weighted difference between them. Differences between rules would be weighted more heavily, while differences between their attributes weighted more lightly, in inverse proportion to their depth (higher level rules generally have wider applicability and are therefore generally more important). If the total difference between the two rule sets exceeds a certain threshold value then the two games are considered to be distinct.

For example, the game on the right below, Tic Tac Toe (4 × 4), would be considered a variant of the game on the left, as the only difference is the board size attribute 4 × 4 as opposed to 3 × 3:

(game Tic-Tac-Toe	(game Tic-Tac-Toe-4×4
(board	(board
(tiling square)	(tiling square)
(size **3 3**)	(size **4 4**)
)	)
(win (in-a-row 3))	(win (in-a-row 3))
)	)

However, the game on the right below, Group 4 would almost certainly be considered a new game in its own right. Not only has the entire (in-a-row 3) clause been replaced by (group 4), giving the game a different goal, but it has been mapped from a 3 × 3 square grid to a hexagonal grid with three cells per side:

(game Tic-Tac-Toe	(game Group-4
(board	(board
(tiling **square**)	(tiling **hex**)
(size 3 3)	(size 3)
)	)
(win (**in-a-row 3**)	(win (**group 4**)
)	)

Game distance becomes important when it comes to gauging the novelty of a new rule set [47].

Chapter 3
The Ludi System

You have to learn the rules of the game.
And then you have to play better than anyone else.

Albert Einstein

Abstract Ludi is a software system written specifically for this project to play, measure and generate new games within the scope of its own game description language. This chapter describes the structure and operation of Ludi, how it understands and plays games, and concludes with an experiment designed to establish player rankings for a set of known source games. The main components of Ludi are:

- *Game description language*: Defines the scope of games.
- *General game player*: Interprets games and coordinates play.
- *Strategy module*: Informs move planning.
- *Criticism module*: Measures game quality.
- *Synthesis module*: Generates new games.

Keywords Ludi · General games · Game description language · General game player · General game system

Figure 3.1 Shows the components of the Ludi general game system, for playing, evaluating and generating new games within the scope of its custom game description language.

3.1 Game Description Language

Central to any general game system is the *game description language* (GDL) that defines the scope of games that it understands. There is a delicate balance between defining a GDL that is powerful and extensible enough to encompass a wide range of known and not-yet-known games, yet also efficient, elegant and comprehensible to human authors.

The most widely used GDL is probably the Zillions Rules File (ZRF) format used for the commercial Zillions of Games application [38]. ZRF authors define

C. Browne, *Evolutionary Game Design*, SpringerBriefs in Computer Science,
DOI: 10.1007/978-1-4471-2179-4_3, © Cameron Browne 2011

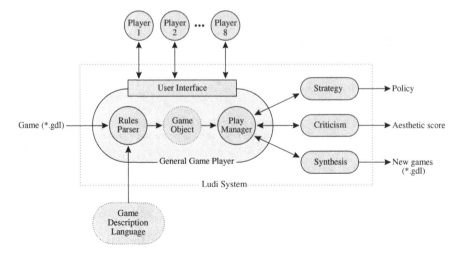

Fig. 3.1 Overview of the Ludi system

games in a Lisp-like syntax using predefined keywords, and may programmatically create complex rule structures through macros. More recently, the Stanford GDL used for the AAAI GGP competitions [24] is a lower level language that defines games using first order logic.

The Ludi GDL is a high level game description language based on the ludemic understanding of games that a human designer would typically employ when conceptualising a game. It is structured to follow the *means-play-ends* model of games introduced earlier, and devised with Kernighan and Pike's [31] principles of good software design in mind:

- simplicity,
- clarity,
- generality, and
- automation.

The following example conveys the essence of the language:

```
(game Tic-Tac-Toe
    (players White Black)
    (board
        (tiling square i-nbors)
        (size 3 3)
    )
    (end (All win (in-a-row 3)))
)
```

Fig. 3.2 Ludeme (rule) tree
for Tic Tac Toe

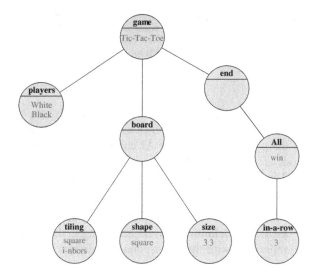

This game (Tic Tac Toe) is played between White and Black on a 3 × 3 square
grid with orthogonal and diagonal adjacency, and is won by the player to make a
line of three pieces of their colour (if any). Unless otherwise stated, it is assumed
that players take turns placing a piece of their colour on an empty board cell each
move. Figure 3.2 shows how this example rule set would be described as a
ludemic rule tree.

The Ludi GDL is a higher level language than the Zillions ZRF and Stanford
GDL. Table 3.1 shows a comparison of the languages based on the number of
tokens required to define Tic Tac Toe and Chess. It can be seen that the Ludi GDL
is more efficient that ZRF and *much* more efficient than the Stanford GDL in terms
of token usage.

Games are easier to express in the Ludi GDL as the complexity of the rules is
hidden in the implementation rather than the language itself. This limits the scope
of the language as only known rules can be used, whereas the lower-level
languages act as building blocks with which new rules can be built. However, the
subset of games allowed by Ludi proved sufficiently rich for the task at hand, and
its hierarchical rule tree structure is ideal for the evolution of rule sets; they
correspond directly to Lisp-style symbolic expressions or *S-expressions* to which
genetic programming (GP) techniques can be readily applied [33].

3.2 General Game Player

The core of the Ludi system is its *general game player* (GGP). General game
players are programmes that can play a range of games well rather than any
particular game expertly. The idea was first proposed several decades ago [46] but

Table 3.1 Token counts for game description languages

	Ludi GDL	ZRF	Stanford GDL
Tic Tac Toe	19	88	384
Chess	325	528	4,392

the first practical GGPs were developed much later [43, 57]. GGPs have recently enjoyed a resurgence of interest as researchers come to realise their potential value to the gaming and broader AI communities, and GGP conferences and competitions are now run annually.

The Ludi GGP interprets and plays games defined in the Ludi GDL. It is implemented in C++ and consists of the following main components:

1. *Rules Parser:* The rules parser loads and parses games defined in the Ludi GDL. If a definition is valid according to the grammar, then the game object is initialised with the corresponding rule tree.
2. *Game Object:* A single game object is maintained for the currently loaded game. This involves keeping a record of the current board state and handling tasks such as the generation of legal moves and testing for terminal conditions.
3. *Play Manager:* Coordinates play for one to eight human and/or artificial players (only two are used for this study). This includes move scheduling, input handling, cycle detection, all players passing, and so on.
4. *User Interface:* The graphical user interface (GUI) presents games and related information graphically to the players, for ease of use.

The Ludi GUI, shown in Fig. 3.3, is functional rather than aesthetic in nature; it presents games uniformly and anonymously so that quality judgments are made on the merits of the games themselves rather than their visual attractiveness. The GUI provides a plain English translation of the current rule set and a tutorial mode to help players understand new games. In tutorial mode, legal placements are marked '+' and legal destination cells for movable pieces are similarly marked '+' when those pieces are clicked on. This level of assistance is important as this project will focus on the creation of new games with possibly complex rules.

Since rule sets are evolved into novel combinations and we cannot rely on the evolutionary process to always produce sensible results, then the rules parser must be robust to all possible rule combinations possible within the GDL. The GGP therefore performs extensive rule checking to ensure that any given GDL file fully describes a legal game, and will gracefully reject any file for which a valid game object cannot be constructed.

3.2.1 Anti-Cycle Measures

Similarly, the play manager must be robust to degenerate situations which may not be obvious from the rules themselves but might emerge during play, such as

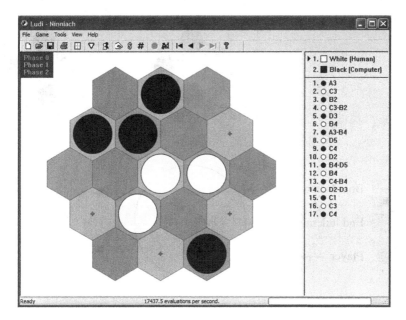

Fig. 3.3 Ludi user interface

infinite cycles that stall progress. This is especially important for Ludi as it must conduct extensive self-play trials without supervision.

The first anti-cycle measure is to terminate the game currently being played if all players pass in succession. If this triggers a win condition then the game is awarded to the appropriate player, otherwise the game is marked as being abandoned (for measurement purposes) and considered a draw between the players.

The second anti-cycle measure is to check whether the board position following each move exactly repeats the previous board position on the same player's turn. Such repetitions are known to Go players as *ko* situations, an example of which is shown in Fig. 3.4. Ludi handles *ko* moves by overlooking them during search lookahead and forbidding them during play.

3.3 Strategy Module

The GGP plans moves for artificial players using standard *alpha beta* adversarial search with 1-ply *move ordering*, *beam width* reduction and *iterative deepening* [50]. Estimated values for non-terminal board positions are provided by the Strategy module using a set of advisors working within certain policies.

Fig. 3.4 A *ko* cycle

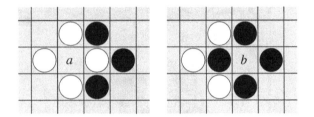

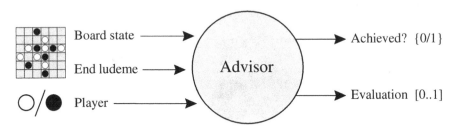

Fig. 3.5 Advisor model

3.3.1 Advisors

Advisors are evaluation functions that represent some narrow but rational view of the board position [21], and express whether a player's position is favorable or unfavorable within this perspective [44].

Each advisor takes as input a board state, end condition and player colour (Fig. 3.5) and returns either of two values depending on the context of the call:

1. An estimate of the board state according to this advisor (range 0–1).
2. A boolean value indicating whether the specified end condition is met.

Advisor objects therefore play a double role as both positional advisors and end condition tests to efficiently use code common to both tasks. The full set of 20 advisors implemented for the Strategy module is listed in Appendix C, and the operation of the *N*-in-a-row advisor is now explained by way of example.

3.3.2 N-*in-a-Row* Advisor

For each piece belonging to the specified player, the total number of possible lines of the required length that pass through that piece are found and the number of pieces along each line counted, giving a *line potential* that indicates how close each possible line is to completion. This value is halved if an opponent's piece blocks one end and halved again if another opponent's piece blocks the other end.

Fig. 3.6 *N*-in-a-row advisor

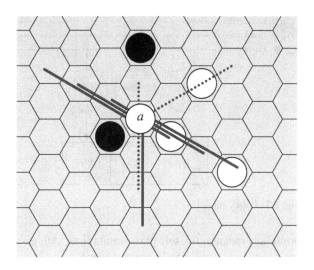

Consider piece *a* in the 4-in-a-row game shown in Fig. 3.6. The line potentials through piece *a* are:

{ 1/4, 2/4, 2/4, 3/4, 1/8, 1/4, 2/8 }

Line potentials are similarly calculated over all pieces belonging to the specified player (duplicates are ignored) and the advisor's final estimate is the combination of these potentials as a union of probabilities:

$$Adv_{nina} = p\left(\cup_{i=1}^{n} L_i\right) \tag{1}$$

The *N*-in-a-row advisor is probably the most successful of all the advisors, allowing fast execution and competent computer play even at low search depths. For a list of all advisors see Appendix C and for further details see Browne [14].

3.3.3 Policies

The contributions from each advisor are combined using a weighted linear function to provide an overall value *E*(*s*) for board state *s*:

$$E(s) = w_1 f_1(s) + w_2 f_2(s) + \ldots + w_n f_n(s) = \sum_{i=1}^{n} w_i f_i(s) \tag{2}$$

where *w* is a vector of weights and $\{f_1(s),\ldots,f_n(s)\}$ the set of advisor functions. The weight vector *w* constitutes a *policy* that describes the relative importance of each advisor for that game (Fig. 3.7).

Although a high level of play cannot be claimed for all games, this advisor/ policy approach proved sufficient for exercising games expressed in the GDL and

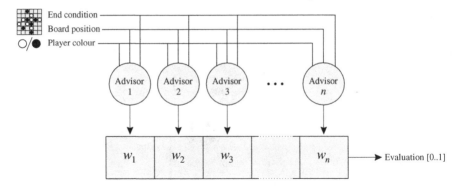

Fig. 3.7 Policy model

providing meaningful self-play simulations. All players—human and artificial—are beginners at any newly created game.

3.3.4 Policy Selection

Only those advisors relevant to the current game are given non-zero weight, to avoid unnecessary processing. Ludi is able to derive a *default policy* for each game based upon its rules and to optimise that policy through self-play using two-membered evolutionary search if required. For example, if a given game has a reach-a-goal objective then the *proximity-to-goal* advisor would automatically be activated while the *mobility* and *influence* advisors may be activated later during policy optimisation, and their relative weights fine-tuned as appropriate.

It is possible in some games for a player to have no specified end condition. This may validly occur when a player's goals are implied by the opponent's end conditions, such as the following Fox & Geese variant in which White wins by reaching the far side of the board but loses if their piece is immobilised, in which case Black wins by implication:

```
(end
     (White win (reach away))
     (White lose (no-move))
)
```

The following default "fight or flight" policy is used for such goalless players:

```
(advisors
     (proxe 1)
     (mobil 1)
     (infl 1)
)
```

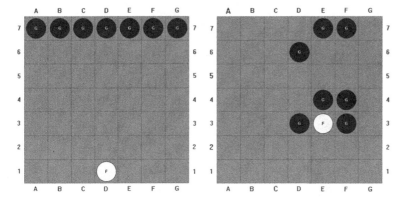

Fig. 3.8 The null policy results in aggressive swarming behaviour

This policy activates the *proximity-to-enemy*, *mobility* and *influence* advisors with equal weight, which has the effect of encouraging pieces to engage the enemy while maximising escape options. For example, Fig. 3.8 shows the swarming behaviour that results from the null policy in a Fox & Geese variant, in which the Black piece (the Geese) can be seen to congregate towards the enemy White piece (the Fox) without unduly cluttering themselves.

3.3.5 Emergent Strategies

Policy optimisation threw up some surprising—and often amusing—emergent strategies. For example, Fig. 3.9 shows an example of degenerate behaviour that emerged during policy optimisation of a stacking game. In this game, new pieces may be added to empty cells or existing pieces moved to an adjacent cell, possibly to stack, with the aim being to achieve three friendly pieces in a row.

Figure 3.9 shows the position with Black to move (top left). Black move *a* blocks the immediate loss by stacking on one of the threatening pieces to hide it, then White replies with stacking move *b*. Move *b* appears reasonable as it removes the Black piece from play, maximising White's line potential while minimising Black's, but proves to be an overly defensive play. Black must add a piece with *c* then White restores the line threat by adding *d*, Black stacks on the threat to hide it with *e*, and this cycle continues ad infinitum (or until the pieces run out) as the central stack grows to absorb all pieces that are played. No board state is repeated in this sequence so the GGP's *ko* mechanism is not applied.

One solution might be to forbid stacking above a certain height, but this would be a rather arbitrary and superficial approach. Instead, a more elegant solution was to apply a small negative *stack* advisor weighting for games in which stacking may occur but is not a winning condition. This anti-stacking mechanism was found to

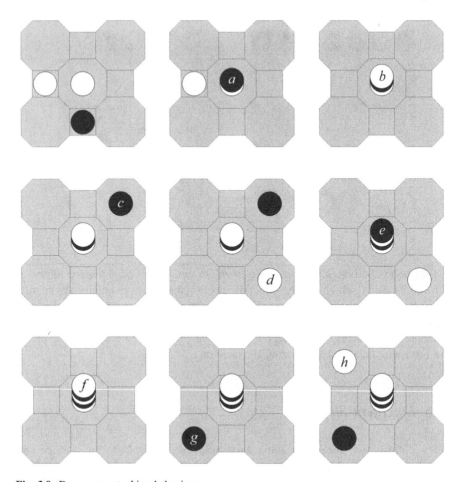

Fig. 3.9 Degenerate stacking behaviour

nudge the AI out of such overly defensive and detrimental stacking behaviour and was incorporated in the default policy for appropriate games.

Other unexpected self-learnt strategies to emerge include a preference for the central cell in Tic Tac Toe, a preference for playing along the sides in a game involving leapfrog capture (side pieces cannot be jumped over), a preference for diagonal movement in some games for which this was beneficial (if not immediately obvious), and so on.

Judicious advisor usage and weighting can therefore be used not only for board state evaluation, but also for discouraging errant behaviour, and even defining subgoals to encourage strategic play in the AI. For example, if a player feels that capturing the Queen is a worthwhile subgoal in Chess, then they can specify the Queen as a target piece in a dummy end condition, add the corresponding advisor and weight it highly.

Table 3.2 Top ten survey
games as ranked by players

Rank	Id	Game
#1	4	Gomoku (hexagonal board, connected move, capture replace)
#2	76	Y
#3	57	Capture 5 (jump capture)
#4	75	Unlur
#5	37	Hex (8 pieces each, unconstrained movement)
#6	61	Form a Group (knight moves, capture replace)
#7	49	Stack 5 (line conversion)
#8	46	Gomoku (move if freedom, surround capture)
#9	0	Breakthrough
#10	35	Hex (hexagonal board)

3.4 Experiment I: Game Ranking

Seventy nine games were defined in the Ludi GDL as an initial data set of inspiring examples [47]. These consisted mostly of test games with no known equivalent devised during the development of the system, in addition to 11 known games (or close approximations of them). Most were viable games that played reasonably well, although several rule sets with pathological flaws were added to give a more complete coverage of the game design space.

The aim of Experiment I was to rank these 79 source games by player preference, to distinguish those games that interest human players from those that do not. This ranking is important for future game measurements.

Method   Experimental subjects were presented with survey software that randomly selected two games from the database of 79, then required them to play both games against the AI and nominate which of the two they found more interesting. Paired comparisons were automatically emailed to the author.

Subjects   57 subjects participated in the survey, recruited from online board gaming groups. All were at least 18 years of age.

Results   Rankings were induced from 628 paired comparisons by a *cross-entropy* (CE) method suggested by Frederic Maire [14]. The 79 sample games were ranked from most preferred to least preferred with a classification rate of 0.8997 (±0.000318), indicating that the derived game rankings were consistent with almost 90% reliability.

Table 3.2 lists the top ten survey games as ranked by survey participants. Each entry is described by the closest known game name with key rule differences noted, but these descriptions are for internal use only; the survey games were presented anonymously to users by their index only.

Chapter 4
Measuring Games

The beauty of a move lies not in its appearance but in the thought behind it.

Siegbert Tarrasch

Abstract One of the key tasks of a general game system such as Ludi is to evaluate the quality of the content that it produces. To this end, Ludi's Criticism module returns an estimated aesthetic score for each candidate games indicating how likely it will be of interest to human players. This estimated score is based on underlying principles of game design and a new aesthetic model that incorporates intrinsic properties of the rule set and extrinsic properties that emerge during play. A number of aesthetic criteria are automatically measured through self-play and combined to give a final score. This chapter describes the aesthetic criteria implemented for Ludi and the evaluation process, and concludes with an experiment conducted to determine whether the predicted aesthetic scores correlate with human player rankings for a given set of games.

Keywords Game quality · Aesthetic measure · Aesthetic criteria · Lead history · Ludi

4.1 Quantifying Quality

The *quality* of a game is the likelihood that it will be of interest to human players. However, game design is something of an art; players generally know whether they enjoy a game or not, but few can articulate the reasons in concrete terms. The first step in measuring a game's quality is in quantifying the underlying principles. As Perlis [45] states:

We measure our understanding (and control) by the extent to which we can mathematize an activity.

C. Browne, *Evolutionary Game Design*, SpringerBriefs in Computer Science,
DOI: 10.1007/978-1-4471-2179-4_4, © Cameron Browne 2011

4.1.1 Game Quality

Game designer Mark Thompson took a significant step towards formalising concepts of game quality by defining four key attributes that a game should possess if it is to have lasting merit [56]:

- *Depth*: Games should hold lasting interest.
- *Clarity*: Their mechanics should not be confusing.
- *Drama*: There should be at least the hope of recovery from bad positions.
- *Decisiveness*: Games should end quickly once a winner is certain.

It is worth distinguishing between strategic and tactical play as this point. *Strategy* is the art of war and concerns the overall management of forces in conflict with an enemy, while *tactics* involve the low-level deployment of these forces to achieve the desired goals. Strategy therefore equates with long-term (global) planning while tactics equate with short-term (local) planning. Abbott observes that the depth of a game depends on how far a player can see down its strategy tree, and that this in turn depends on the clarity of the game [1].

Thompson also points out that games may be viewed as sequences of logic puzzles that players pose to each other, and hence a good game should readily yield such puzzle positions. Taking this analogy further, puzzle inventor Sam Loyd observed that his goal was to compose puzzles whose solution require a first move that is contrary to what 999 players out of 1,000 would propose [26]. This notion of *obfuscation* ties in neatly with the combinatorial game player's pleasure in playing apparently inconsequential moves that hide a more subtle threat, laying traps and trying to outsmart the opponent.

Other proposed indicators of quality proposed include *interestingness* [4], *uncertainty* [29], *interaction* [13] and *tension* [34]. Uncertainty in the outcome of a game is of paramount importance if players are to maintain a vested interest in it. *Originality* in design is also of great importance, as games should continue to surprise the player.

Just as mathematicians strive for beautiful, aesthetically meaningful abstractions [23], we are concerned not with the sensual beauty of games but their intellectual appeal; the elegance of the rules, how well they complement each other, and the quality of the competition they produce. Contrary to Ellis [20], the absence of flaws is a precondition for beauty in this case.

4.1.2 Aesthetic Measure

George Birkhoff introduced the concept of *aesthetic measure*, which involves the calculation of an aesthetic value for a given object as a function of certain *aesthetic criteria* [8]. This approach was later extended to a complete *algorithmic aesthetics* system for the design and criticism of aesthetically meaningful visual objects by Stiny and Gips [54]. Similar principles can be applied to the aesthetic

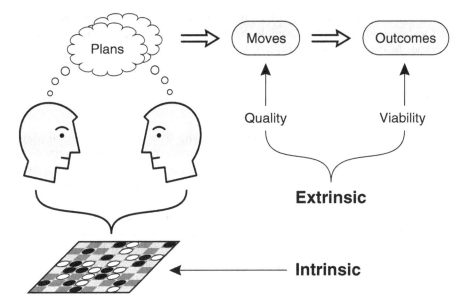

Fig. 4.1 Aesthetic model of games

measurement of games; in this case, the interpretation of an object (game) will be a set of aesthetic measurements derived through self-play, and the output of the algorithm will be a single predicted aesthetic value.

Stiny and Gips distinguish between *constructive* and *evocative* modes for the understanding of objects within this system. In constructive mode objects are understood by the rules of their construction, and in evocative mode they are understood by the associations, ideas or emotions they evoke. We focus on the evocative mode of understanding, as we wish to create games that players find interesting to play without making any assumptions about the underlying rules.

4.1.3 Aesthetic Model

Figure 4.1 shows the player-centric aesthetic model of games devised for this study, based on the earlier model of creativity in games that distinguishes between aspects of *design* and *play* (Fig. 1.2). While it is possible to measure some aspects of a game's design directly through its equipment and rules, it is of course a much more difficult task to quantitatively measure the players' strategic plans over the course of a game as an indicator of their engagement with it. However, we can do the next best thing which is to measure the moves that the players make (the tangible realisations of those plans) and the outcome of each game (the overall effect of those moves).

This aesthetic model distinguishes between *intrinsic* properties based on the rules and equipment, and less tangible *extrinsic* properties based on the moves and outcomes of the resulting games.

4.1.4 Operation

Aesthetic measurements are made for each game over a number of self-play trials *G*. The first few moves of each trial are made randomly to encourage a more thorough exploration of the move search space, just as many computer game tournaments use random *opening ballots* to balance games and encourage variety in play. An even number of random moves is made so that any first move advantage is not entirely lost, and these initial random moves are excluded from the aesthetic measurements. Each game *g* thus has a total number of moves M_g composed of a number of random starting moves M_{gr} followed by a number of intelligent (i.e. non-random) moves in M_{gi} in standard play, as follows:

$$M_g = M_{gr} + M_{gi} \tag{4.1}$$

A number of aesthetic criteria are applied to provide an aesthetic value based on these self-play trials.

4.2 Aesthetic Criteria

A total of 57 aesthetic criteria were implemented for Ludi, classified as being either *intrinsic*, *viability* or *quality*, as follows:

- 16 × intrinsic,
- 11 × viability, and
- 30 × quality.

Each criterion returns a floating point value in the range −1 to 1, indicating the estimated prevalence of that criterion over *G* self-play trials. While researchers of more popular games such as Go and Chess often have access to large databases of expert games for positional analysis and machine learning purposes, general game researchers typically do not have this luxury, and Ludi is no exception. Most of the games produces will not have been played or even seen before, so any required game records must be generated through self-play.

Each criterion is given a relative weighting, and the weighted sum of all 57 criteria results yields an estimated aesthetic score A_s, which is the single value output by the Criticism module in response to each game:

$$A_s = \left(\sum_{i=0}^{C-1} A_i w_i \right) + w_c \tag{4.2}$$

The aesthetic weightings w_i provide an aesthetic profile for each game, while the bias term w_c improves the accuracy of the overall correlation. Criteria with a zero weighting are not invoked, for efficiency.

Some criteria are significantly slower to measure than others and require an additional G trials to be run in different modes, for example criteria related to puzzle detection or those that gauge the game's susceptibility to degenerate playing styles such overly random, defensive, obstructive or selfish players. It is therefore important to identify those criteria that are not necessary and set their weight to zero.

This set of 57 criteria does not represent a universal or canonical set of features with which all games may be measured, but rather a fair selection based on observation, experience and prior work. A few of the more important criteria are now described by way of example; the complete list is given in Appendix D, and for further details including implementation notes see Browne [14].

4.2.1 Intrinsic Criteria

Intrinsic criteria—those based on rules and equipment—are the easiest to measure, but are less useful for indicating game quality than they are for specifying personal feature preferences. Intrinsic criteria include aspects such as whether a game's rules involve a particular mechanism or goal type, and are measured before any self-play trials are run. They typically return zero to indicate the absence of a rule or one to indicate its presence.

4.2.2 Viability Criteria

Viability criteria—those based on game outcomes—are robust and useful for quickly identifying those games that are fundamentally playable and produce at least some degree of balanced contest between its players. They are the system's first line of defense in filtering out legal but deeply flawed games.

Four criteria emerged as especially useful at quickly identifying flawed games ($wins_W$ = White wins, $wins_B$ = Black wins, and $wins_1$ = wins by player 1):

1. *Completion*: Games should produce more victories than draws. A low completion rate indicates a flawed game that is either drawish or tends to exceed the maximum move limit. The completion rate A_{comp} is given by the total sum of games won by either player as a ratio of all games G:

$$A_{comp} = (wins_w + wins_B)/G \qquad (4.3)$$

2. *Balance*: Games should not favour either colour. The balance A_{bal} is given by the absolute ratio of difference in wins between the two players:

$$A_{bal} = 1 - \frac{|wins_w - wins_B|}{wins_w + wins_B} \qquad (4.4)$$

3. *Advantage*: Games should not favour the first or second player. The advantage A_{adv} is given by the absolute ratio of games that the first player wins, above or below the expected 50%:

$$A_{adv} = \frac{|wins_1 - (wins_w + wins_B)/2|}{(wins_w + wins_B)/2} \qquad (4.5)$$

4. *Duration*: Games should end after a reasonable number of moves; they should not end after only a few moves but nor should they be excessively long or indecisive. Duration is given by the average absolute deviation of each trial game length M_g from the preferred game length M_{pref}:

$$A_{durn} = \sum_{g=1}^{G} \frac{|M_{pref} - M_g|}{M_{pref}} \Big/ G \qquad (4.6)$$

A preferred game length of $M_{pref} = 60$ moves was chosen for all games, based on the observation that two human players spending 30 s per move would complete such a game in 30 min on average, a figure that experience suggests is reasonable (note that Ludi generally plays much faster than this). This value was not adjusted for smaller boards otherwise shorter games would have been rewarded, when we really wish to reward deep, involved passages of play emerging from simpler rule sets, in the true spirit of combinatorial game design.

Self-play trials that exceed twice the preferred game length are halted and abandoned as draws, so that indecisive games that might otherwise not reach a conclusion are caught within a reasonable time.

4.2.3 Quality Criteria

Quality criteria are the most subtle and difficult to measure, as they attempt to gauge players' engagement with a game through the secondary evidence afforded by their moves. They typically attempt to measure trends in play during the self-play trials using *lead histories* as shown in Fig. 4.2. The white and black dots indicate the estimated positional strength of the respective player following each move, while the thick line represents the difference between the estimates of the eventual winner (in this case White) and loser (in this case Black) following each move. This provides a useful profile of the players'

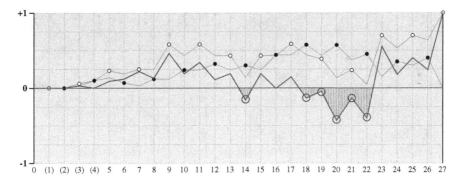

Fig. 4.2 Lead history of a dramatic game

relative fortunes throughout each game, with areas in which the lead line drops below the x axis indicating sections in which the eventual winner finds themself in a trailing position.

For example, it can be seen that White trails for much of the second half before suddenly winning this game, indicating a dramatic turnaround that marks this game as one of potential interest. Things look especially bad for White at moves 19 and 21 where they are in a negative position *after their move*, until killer move 23 turns the game around.

The move numbers for the first few moves of each game are bracketed to indicate that they are random and should be excluded from the aesthetic calculations.

4.2.3.1 Drama

This example highlights the notion of *drama*, as players should have at least a hope of recovering from bad positions if they are to maintain a vested interest in a game. The drama criterion A_{drav} measures the degree to which the winner of each game suffers a negative lead:

$$A_{drav} = \sum_{g=1}^{G} \left(\frac{E_w(m_n) < E_l(m_n)\{\sqrt{E_l(m_n) - E_w(m_n)}}{\underset{[M_{gr} + 1 \le n \le M_g - 1]}{count}} (E_w(m_n) < E_l(m_n)) \right) \bigg/ G \qquad (4.7)$$

where $E_w(m_n)$ represents the board evaluation for the eventual winner at move n and $E_l(m_n)$ represents the board evaluation for the eventual loser at move n. This equation measures the average number of moves that the eventual winner of each game spends in a negative position, and the severity of each such position.

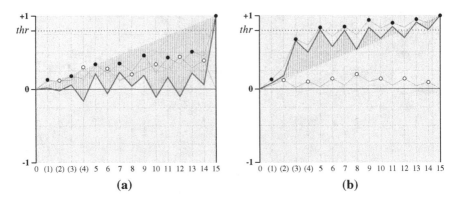

Fig. 4.3 Lead histories of uncertain (**a**) and certain (**b**) games

4.2.3.2 Uncertainty

The outcome of each game should remain *uncertain* for as long as possible if all players are to maintain a vested interest in it. Figure 4.3a shows an uncertain game in which neither player develops a strong advantage until its conclusion, while Fig. 4.3b shows a certain game in which the eventual winner takes a strong early lead and keeps it; this will be an unsatisfying game for the losing player.

The uncertainty criterion A_{uncl} measures the degree to which the estimated lead value for each move falls above or below the expected average:

$$A_{uncl} = \sum_{s=0}^{s-1} \left(\min\left(1, t - \left(\sum_{g=1}^{G} E_{co}\left(M_{tMg}\right) \right) \bigg/ G \right) \right) \bigg/ S \qquad (4.8)$$

The amount of uncertainty is indicated by the area enclosed by the lead history plot and an imaginary line drawn from (0, 0) to (M, 1). A number of samples $S = 100$ are made at regular intervals t across the completed game history, and the average distance measured between this interpolation line and $E_{co}(m_{tMg})$ the estimated lead value at time t. Samples that fall below the interpolation line indicate greater uncertainty.

4.2.3.3 Lead Change

Lead change is simply the tendency for the lead to change over the course of a game. This is distinct from drama as it is the frequency of lead change that counts in this case, not the accumulated time that the eventual winner spend in a trailing position. Figure 4.4 shows a game with four lead changes, indicated by zero crossings in the lead plot (circled).

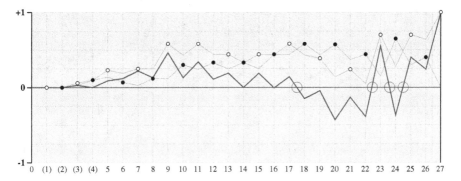

Fig. 4.4 Lead changes throughout a game

The lead change criterion A_{lead} measures the number of zero crossings in the lead plot as a fraction of total intelligent (i.e. non-random) moves M_{gi}:

$$A_{lead} = \sum_{g=1}^{G} \left(\frac{\sum_{n=M_g+1}^{M_g} leader(m_n) \neq leader(m_{n-1})\{^1_0\}}{M_{gi} - 1} \right) \Big/ G \qquad (4.9)$$

4.2.3.4 Killer Moves

Players often like to play *killer moves* that significantly improve their positions and swing the course of the game. Again, these are closely related to drama as they can allow a trailing player to suddenly gain the upper hand.

Figure 4.5 shows a killer move m_{23} that dramatically swings the game in White's favour. Note that neither the increase in White's evaluation or the decrease in Black's evaluation is especially dramatic, the swing is a combination of both.

The killer moves criterion A_{km} measures the move per game that gives the greater relative gain for the mover:

$$A_{km} = \frac{\sum_{g=1}^{G} \displaystyle{\max_{[M_{gr} \leq n \leq M_g - 1]}} [E_c(m_n) - E_o(m_n)] - [E_c(m_{n-1}) - E_o(m_{n-1})]}{G}$$

$$(4.10)$$

where E_c is the board evaluation for the current mover and E_o is the board evaluation for the current opponent on the specified move.

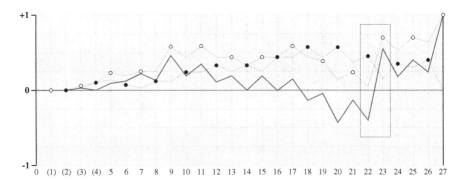

Fig. 4.5 Killer move m_{23}

4.2.3.5 Permanence

However, too many killer moves in a game can make it unstable and chaotic, and ultimately meaningless for players. It is therefore generally good for most moves to have some degree of *permanence* so that the opponent cannot immediately recover to negate the effect of every move.

For example, Fig. 4.6 shows a game in which White makes two moves, m_9 and m_{23}, from which Black immediately recovers with their next move. Thus moves in this game are quite impermanent, especially given that the large advantage gained by m_{23} is immediately negated (the total size of the swing and recovery is relevant). By contrast, the game shown in Fig. 4.5 includes a killer White move m_{23} from which Black does not immediately recover, hence the moves in this game have greater permanence.

The permanence criterion A_{perm} measures the average change in board evaluation over each triplet of moves $\{m_{n-2}, m_{n-1}, m_n\}$ and incorporates the magnitude of the evaluation difference of the intervening move m_{n-1}:

$$A_{perm} = \sum_{g=1}^{G} \left(\frac{\sum_{n=M_{gr}+1}^{M_g-1} [E_{co}(m_n) - E_{oc}(m_{n-1})] - [E_{oc}(m_{n-1}) - E_{co}(m_{n-2})]}{M_{gi} - 2} \right) \Bigg/ G$$

(4.11)

where E_{co} is the difference in board evaluations between the current mover and the opponent and E_{oc} is the difference in board evaluations between the opponent and the current mover on the specified move.

It can be seen that these quality criteria are more subtle, abstract and difficult to measure than the viability criteria, but they are essential for estimating the quality of viable games. While the viability criteria filter out unplayable games with broad strokes, the quality criteria allow finer distinctions.

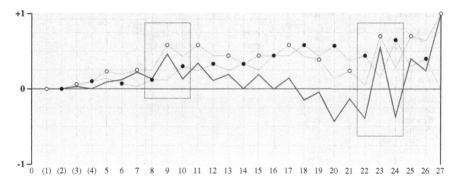

Fig. 4.6 Quick recoveries lack permanence

4.3 Experiment II: Game Measurement

The purpose of experiment II was to determine whether the player rankings induced for the 79 source games in Experiment I could be correlated with their aesthetic measurements, and, if so, what is the minimal criteria set that may safely be assigned non-zero weight.

4.3.1 Method

Each of the 57 aesthetic criteria were measured for the 79 sample games through automated self-play trials, conducted on two Windows desktop machines over a period of two weeks. Some supervision was required to narrow the beam search for slower games, in order to finish the measurements within a reasonable time.

4.3.2 Results

The aesthetic measurements were correlated with player rankings using linear regression and standard leave-one-out cross-validation, to give $corr_r$ the correlation between game ranking and aesthetic score. Figure 4.7 shows the relative correlation weightings over all 57 criteria.

Table 4.1 compares correlation results when the criteria are applied by category. A baseline correlation of 0.426 is found when using all 57 criteria as predictors. It can be seen that the intrinsic criteria in isolation are poor predictors of game ranking (0.115) but that the quality criteria perform relatively well (0.437) and viability criteria even better (0.609) as predictors of game ranking.

However, better results can be obtained using combinations of more relevant criteria. The best set of predictors found involved 17 criteria drawn from all three

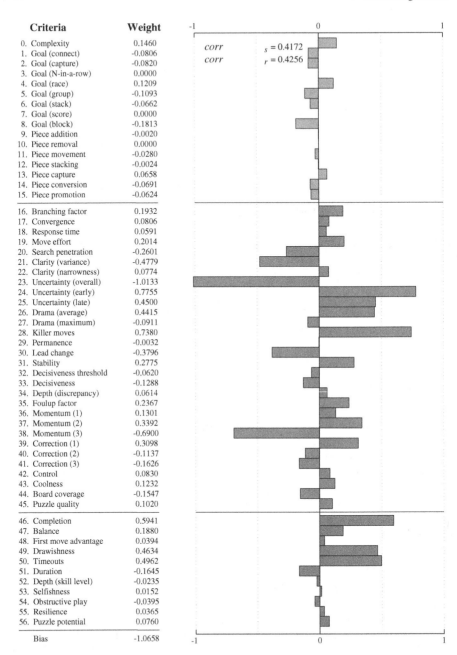

Criteria	Weight
0. Complexity	0.1460
1. Goal (connect)	-0.0806
2. Goal (capture)	-0.0820
3. Goal (N-in-a-row)	0.0000
4. Goal (race)	0.1209
5. Goal (group)	-0.1093
6. Goal (stack)	-0.0662
7. Goal (score)	0.0000
8. Goal (block)	-0.1813
9. Piece addition	-0.0020
10. Piece removal	0.0000
11. Piece movement	-0.0280
12. Piece stacking	-0.0024
13. Piece capture	0.0658
14. Piece conversion	-0.0691
15. Piece promotion	-0.0624
16. Branching factor	0.1932
17. Convergence	0.0806
18. Response time	0.0591
19. Move effort	0.2014
20. Search penetration	-0.2601
21. Clarity (variance)	-0.4779
22. Clarity (narrowness)	0.0774
23. Uncertainty (overall)	-1.0133
24. Uncertainty (early)	0.7755
25. Uncertainty (late)	0.4500
26. Drama (average)	0.4415
27. Drama (maximum)	-0.0911
28. Killer moves	0.7380
29. Permanence	-0.0032
30. Lead change	-0.3796
31. Stability	0.2775
32. Decisiveness threshold	-0.0620
33. Decisiveness	-0.1288
34. Depth (discrepancy)	0.0614
35. Foulup factor	0.2367
36. Momentum (1)	0.1301
37. Momentum (2)	0.3392
38. Momentum (3)	-0.6900
39. Correction (1)	0.3098
40. Correction (2)	-0.1137
41. Correction (3)	-0.1626
42. Control	0.0830
43. Coolness	0.1232
44. Board coverage	-0.1547
45. Puzzle quality	0.1020
46. Completion	0.5941
47. Balance	0.1880
48. First move advantage	0.0394
49. Drawishness	0.4634
50. Timeouts	0.4962
51. Duration	-0.1645
52. Depth (skill level)	-0.0235
53. Selfishness	0.0152
54. Obstructive play	-0.0395
55. Resilience	0.0365
56. Puzzle potential	0.0760
Bias	-1.0658

$corr_s = 0.4172$

$corr_r = 0.4256$

Fig. 4.7 Correlation weightings over all aesthetic criteria

Table 4.1 Correlation by criteria type

Criteria	$Corr_r$
All (57)	0.426
Intrinsic (16)	0.115
Quality (30)	0.437
Viability (11)	0.609
Best set (17)	0.828
Best set (16)	0.799

Criteria	Weight
5. Goal (group)	0.0818
6. Goal (stack)	-0.0804
8. Goal (block)	-0.1055
13. Piece capture	0.0585
17. Convergence	-0.0221
21. Clarity (variance)	-0.3763
25. Uncertainty (late)	0.2023
26. Drama (average)	0.2167
28. Killer moves	0.3585
29. Permanence	0.1027
30. Lead change	-0.2769
32. Decisiveness threshold	0.1311
36. Momentum (1)	0.1244
39. Correction (1)	0.1622
45. Puzzle quality	0.0826
46. Completion	0.0788
51. Duration	-0.0907
Bias	-0.2576

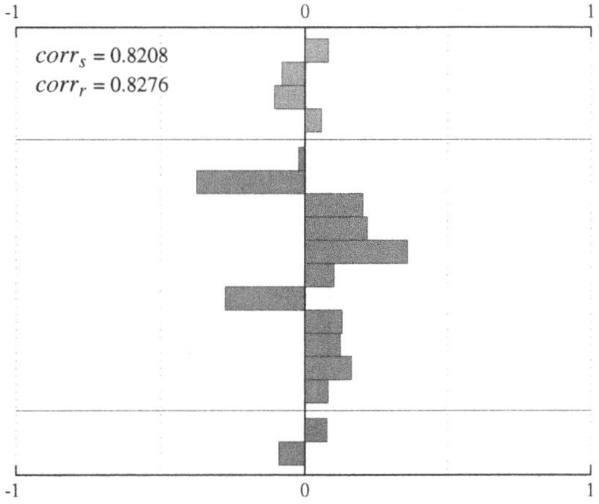

$corr_s = 0.8208$
$corr_r = 0.8276$

Fig. 4.8 Correlation weightings of the set of best 17 predictors

categories and proved to be an excellent predictor of game ranking, with a 0.828 correlation (± 0.371 at the 95% confidence level). The correlation weightings of these best 17 predictors are shown Fig. 4.8. This set was found using another CE method due to Frederic Maire [14].

The relative importance of each of these predictors is indicated in Fig. 4.9, based on the increase in error when each is removed from the set. Six of these criteria stand out as most important:

• uncertainty,
• lead change (negative correlation),
• permanence,
• killer moves,
• completion, and
• duration.

The survey participants appear to prefer stable games with uncertain outcomes that end within a reasonable number of moves, and in which strong moves are reasonably permanent. Lead change is distinct from drama as it refers to lead change frequency.

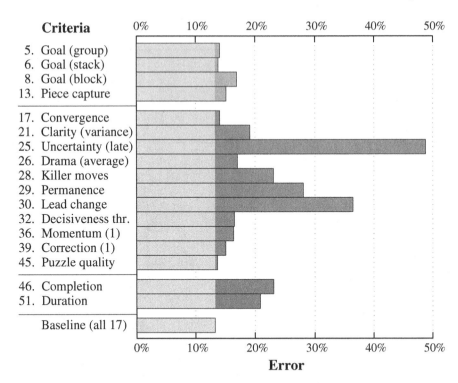

Fig. 4.9 Relative contributions of the best 17 predictors

These results support hypothesis I: *That there exist fundamental (and measurable) indicators of game quality*, at least for this group of subjects and this set of combinatorial games.

Note that the "puzzle quality" criterion was later removed to produce a best set of 16 predictors with a significant speed advantage but negligible loss of accuracy (0.799). This was the set subsequently used for aesthetic evaluations.

Chapter 5
Evolving Games

You may invent your own men and assign them arbitrary
powers. You may design your own boards... The possibilities
are endless.

Henry Kuttner, *Chessboard Planet*

Abstract The description of combinatorial games as hierarchical rule sets equivalent to symbolic expressions (S-expressions) makes them ideal for manipulation through genetic programming (GP) techniques. This chapter introduces the standard GP approach then goes on to describe how this method is adapted for the evolution of new rule sets in the Synthesis module of the Ludi general game system. The chapter concludes with an experiment designed to gauge the system's success in producing games that human players find interesting.

Keywords Genetic programing · Evolutionary approach · Game design · Ludi · Intron · Rule safety · Viability filter

5.1 Computer Aided Game Design

Pell has previously demonstrated the automated generation of Chess-like games using a method of *constrained stochastic context-free generation*, in which the user specifies a number of parameters and games are created by making statistical choices at each decision point in the grammar according to these parameters [44]. Similarly, Rolle's Morphling allows the user to interactively experiment with rule variations of a game according to certain rules [48].

Games created by these systems fall within the constructive mode of understanding of Stiny and Gips' [54] algorithmic aesthetics model as they are directly constructed according to certain rules. These systems typify *computer-aided game design* in which the system acts as an assistant in their creative task.

However, we wish to go a step further and hand the creative responsibility over to the system more fully. The evocative mode of understanding is more appropriate in this case, as we wish to find new games that human players find interesting based on their preferences rather than any knowledge of the underlying

C. Browne, *Evolutionary Game Design*, SpringerBriefs in Computer Science,
DOI: 10.1007/978-1-4471-2179-4_5, © Cameron Browne 2011

rules; the system must determine which rule rules are important and which rule combinations work well together. Adopting the evocative mode also increases the likelihood that unexpected rule combinations and behaviours will emerge. To this end a genetic programming approach was chosen to search the game design space.

5.1.1 Genetic Programming

Genetic programming (GP) uses methods borrowed from natural evolution, such as crossover and mutation, to produce computer programmes that represent particular solutions in the overall solution space [33]. Like other evolutionary approaches, GP balances the *exploration* of the design space with the *exploitation* of existing knowledge [5]. GP is typically applied to problems represented as functional *symbolic expressions* or S-expressions, so is particularly apt for rule sets defined in Ludi's hierarchical game description language. A game's *genotype* is its rule set and its *phenotype* is the resulting contest manifested as the moves that the players make.

Content generated by GP methods will typically include some code fragments that do not affect the fitness of the individual. Such useless code fragments are called *introns* [41] and represent recessive genetic material that does not manifest in the phenotype of the individual. The *effective size* of an individual is defined as the number of nodes that constitute working code, while the *absolute size* of an individual is the total number of nodes including introns. Code is deemed to be "working" if it affects the fitness of the individual in any way.

Introns can cause *bloat* in individuals if allowed to go unchecked [55] with their absolute size increasingly outweighing their effective size. However, [41] point to some positive benefits of introns, and have shown how they can be explicitly introduced to improve the search. Firstly, they can help preserve highly fit building blocks within an individual, and secondly they can protect the individual itself almost entirely against the destructive nature of crossover. Most importantly, introns affect the crossover probability of nodes within the individual.

Crossover operations that produce inferior offspring are described as *destructive crossover*, while crossover operations that produce offspring that improve on the parents are described as *constructive crossover*. Some *parsimony pressure* is usually applied to GP populations to reduce the total population size in order to reduce the computational overhead and improve the search focus. Such pressure can be applied by only keeping offspring that improve upon their parents [53], which has the effect of raising the average fitness of the population at the expense of genetic diversity. Individual parsimony may be achieved by parsing individuals to reduce the presence of introns and optimise the absolute size of individuals.

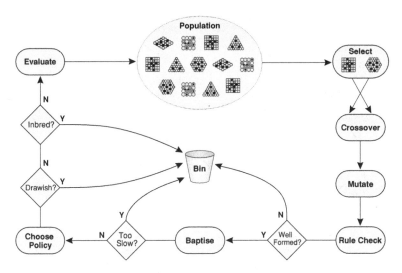

Fig. 5.1   The game life cycle

5.2 Evolutionary Game Design

Ludi uses a standard GP approach to create new games except that parsimony pressure is relaxed; all valid offspring are kept regardless of fitness and none are optimised. Fitness determines order rather than survival, to encourage genetic diversity and the emergence of novel rule combinations. This means that even weak individuals may contribute to future generations, in case their introns harbour partial rule combinations that might prove fruitful in other contexts.

Evolution continues until a given time limit is reached or the desired number of new games created. The basic process is summarised in Fig. 5.1 and explained below. Note that the aim of this process is to produce a wide range of interesting individuals rather than a single optimal individual; it is the search for novel and harmonious rule combinations.

Population The population is initialised with a number of known games to encourage well-formed offspring, as strictly random rule combinations are most unlikely to produce viable games. Members of the population each have a unique name and remain sorted by estimated aesthetic value throughout the process. The initial population may be described as the *inspiring set* for the process, that is the knowledge base of known examples which drives the computation [47].

Parent Selection For each iteration, two parents are selected from the population using *stochastic universal sampling* [6]. This method draws samples from the entire range but selects fitter individuals more often, encouraging genetic diversity while maintaining a reasonable standard of fitness.

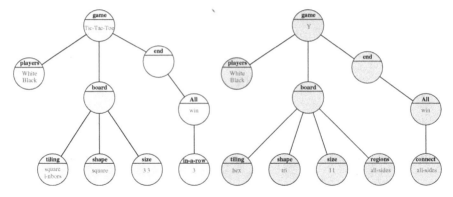

Fig. 5.2 Parent games: Tic Tac Toe and Y

For example, stochastic universal sampling might choose Tic Tac Toe and Y as the two parent games (Fig. 5.2):

(*game* Tic-Tac-Toe	(*game* Y
(*players* White Black	(*players* White Black)
(*board*	(*board*
(*tiling square i-nbors*)	(*tiling hex*)
(*shape square*)	(*shape tri*)
(*size* 3 3)	(*size* 11)
)	(*regions all-sides*)
(*end* (All *win*	)
(*in-a-row* 3))	(*end* (All *win*
)	(*connect all-sides*))
)	)
	)

Recombination The rule sets of the two parents are then *crossed over* to produce a child game in the standard GP manner [33]. One of the parents is chosen at random to act as a *template* [35] and elements crossed over from the second parent with 10% likelihood. Elements are only crossed over to elements with which they are compatible, giving a weak form of *strong typing* [40] that encourages the creation of well-formed children. The hierarchical structure of game described in the Ludi GDL is ideal for this purpose.

Figure 5.3 shows the recombination of the example games Tic Tac Toe and Y into a single child. Tic Tac Toe was chosen as the child's template, the Y *board*

Fig. 5.3 Recombination
using crossover

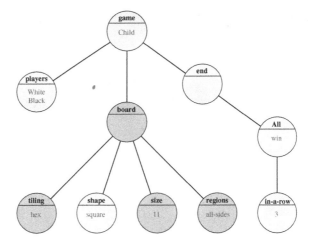

element was crossed over into it, then the original *shape* element from Tic Tac
Toe was crossed over back into it:

```
(game Child
    (players White Black
    (board
      (tiling hex)
      (shape square)
      (size 11)
      (regions all-sides)
    )
    (end (All win (in-a-row 3))))
)
```

Mutation   Each element of the child is then visited and *mutated* with a 10%
likelihood. Each mutation may involve:

• changing the element type,
• removing a subelement,
• adding a subelement,
• changing an attribute value,
• removing an attribute, and/or
• adding an attribute.

   Context-dependent constraints are again employed to ensure that changes are
compatible with element type, and that deleted items are replaced with default
values where needed. Some *repair functions* [39] are used to correct obvious
errors, but mutations are otherwise unconstrained for the sake of genetic diversity.

   When changing an element type, the new element is chosen at random from
those available, except for the following items whose selection is biased by predefined frequency tables:

Fig. 5.4 Child mutation

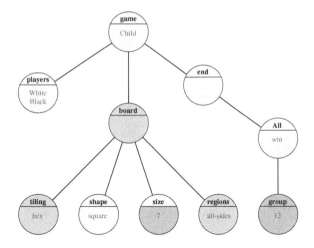

- Trapeziums are less frequent than other hexagonal board shapes.
- The ratio of *win/lose/draw* outcome qualifiers is 8:4:1.
- The *no-move* end condition is 1/4 as likely to occur as other types.
- The ratio of *and/or/if/not/xor* logical operators is 4:4:1:1:1.

Special care is taken to maintain the correct tree structure when mutations involve any of the logical operators {*and/or/if/not/xor*}. For instance, the removal of an *or* rule will remove all of its arguments, and the addition of an *and* rule will randomly create extra rule arguments as necessary.

If an element is changed to a logical operator, then that element becomes the operator's first argument. For instance (*group*) might mutate to (*not* (*group*)) or (*xor* (*group*) (*no-move*)).

Starting positions are handled separately as games generally benefit from symmetrical, balanced starting positions which are unlikely to occur at random. Most *place* mutations are therefore symmetrical and include predefined patterns such as opposed edges with a random number of rows or opposed corners (first and last cell), although some random placements are also made for the sake of diversity.

End condition mutation is constrained to generally favour balanced end conditions, although some unbalance in end conditions is also allowed.

Figure 5.4 shows two typical mutations applied to the example child game. Firstly, the board *size* attribute is changed from 11 to 7. Secondly, the *in-a-row* element is replaced with a *group* element with an attribute of 12:

```
(game Child
    (players White Black
    (board
```

```
        (tiling hex)
        (shape square)
        (size 7)
        (regions all-sides)
    )
    (end (All win (group 12)))
)
```

Baptism Each child is given a short name unique to the population, using a Markov chain algorithm based upon letter triplet frequencies found within a list of source words [31].

Ludi uses a list of Tolkien-style names from the public domain computer game *Angband* [25] as its input. This list only contains 601 entries yet provided short, well-formed and interesting names that are unlikely to be shared by any existing games. Other word lists were tried, including dictionaries of classical Latin and Greek words, but these proved orders of magnitude larger and generally provided less satisfactory results. Typical names for games generated by process include:

- Oroth,
- Galdal,
- Etherond,
- Kemeneth,
- Valindor,
- Bered,
- Mor, and so on.

Any name clashes that occur when merging populations from different evolutionary runs are resolved simply by renaming the offenders.

5.2.1 Quality Assurance

Each child game then undergoes a series of validity checks.

Rule Safety The child is tested for *rule safety* [35] by invoking the GGP to instantiate the corresponding game object to exploit its rigorous error checking systems. For example, Fig. 5.5 indicates that the child game developed in the examples has two problematic rules. The combination of a *hex* tiling with a *square* board shape constitutes a *rule clash* as that combination is not supported by the GGP, while the (*regions all-sides*) element constitutes a *vestigial rule* as this is a throwback to the parents that is irrelevant to the child:

```
(game Child
    (players White Black
    (board
        (tiling hex)
        (shape square)
```

Fig. 5.5 A rule clash (*left*)
and a vestigial rule (*right*)

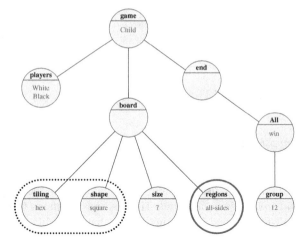

Fig. 5.6 Correction of the
square shape to *rhombus*

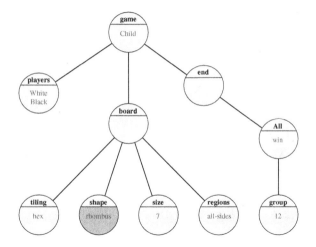

```
        (size 7)
        (regions all-sides)
    )
    (end (All win (group 12)))
)
```

It would be a simple matter to correct the rule clash by say replacing the *square*
board shape with a *rhombus*, as shown in Fig. 5.6:

```
(game Child
    (players White Black
    (board
        (tiling hex)
        (shape rhombus)
```

```
      (size 7)
      (regions all-sides )
  )
   (end (All win (group 12)))
)
```

However, it would be a difficult and time consuming task to plan for, detect and correct all possible degenerate cases within the language, especially given the complexity of play which may emerge. Instead, it is easier and more efficient to just discard any degenerate child and move onto the next generation; the creation of new children is very fast.

Introns It would be tempting at this point to remove vestigial rules such as the superfluous (*regions all-sides*) element in the example, as minimal rule sets lead to "refined, tight, classy little games" [18] and are generally more elegant and easier for human readers to interpret.

However, preliminary tests revealed the importance of such introns to the success of the evolutionary process, as they act as dormant genes which pass unused through generations only to reach their full potential in combination with other rules in later generations. It is unlikely that truly innovative rule combinations will emerge, fully formed, from the crossover and mutation of optimised, parsimonious rule sets.

Introns are therefore tolerated as partial rule stubs that encourage genetic diversity and retained if they do not actually break the game. This design choice was validated by the number of serendipitous rule combinations that emerged during evolution which would have been extremely unlikely to occur with stricter rule optimisation; Yavalath provides a striking example.

In addition, it can be difficult to gauge the impact that culling an apparently superfluous rule will have on a game. For example, a piece with no movement may appear superfluous but could have a subtle but necessary impact on the game through its placement. Detecting whether any rule can safely be removed would be possible but prohibitively time consuming at this point; such optimisation is best left as a post-processing step if a game appears to be of interest and more time can be devoted to it.

Ludi hence foregoes the rule optimisations that would typically be performed at this stage of a GP process. As Perlis [45] observes: *Optimization hinders evolution.* As an aside, assaulting the rule parser with essentially random rule combinations proved a useful method of stress testing the system to reveal bugs.

Speed Test Each child game was timed at search plies of 1, 2, 3 and 4 and discarded if move planning exceeded 15 s per move. This somewhat draconian measure ensures that slower games don't unduly hold up the evolutionary process.

Speeds were improved by limiting board size to the following:

- 8 × 8 square,
- 11 × 11 rhombus,
- 11-per-side triangular,

- 5-per-side hexagonal, and
- 7-per-side trapezium.

One concern is that these self-imposed size and speed limits will filter out more complex games, typically those on larger boards with more pieces and greater branching factors, and risk producing simple children only. However, the results from Experiment II suggest that game quality does not depend on branching factor (and by implication board size) and the surviving games proved more than sufficient for meaningful play. If anything, this preference for the smaller and simpler resonates more strongly with the abstract game designer's ideal of producing elegant games in which simple rules combine harmoniously to produce complex move decisions, rather than seeking complexity in sheer volume of numbers.

Policy Choice An initial policy is then chosen for the child in preparation for self-play trials. As full policy optimisation is time consuming and not always successful, it is preferable to instead leverage the policy information available from the parents; these are a good starting point given that the parent policies were optimised for the rule sets from which the child was derived.

There are three readily available policies likely to be relevant to the child:

- the child's default policy,
- parent A's policy, and
- parent B's policy.

These may be combined by adding the component weights to produce *hybrid policies*, giving a total of seven combinations likely to be relevant to the child:

- default,
- parent A,
- parent B,
- parent A + parent B,
- parent A + default,
- parent B + default, and
- parent A + parent B + default.

Each policy is played twice against each other (one start each) and the most successful chosen for the child. The child is discarded if these selection games take too long or more than half fail to produce a winner.

The chosen policy is unlikely to be optimal for the child game. However, its function at this stage of the evolutionary process is to allow the completion of legal games for measurement purposes rather than achieving a high standard of play; a better policy may be chosen later if the game proves to be of interest.

Inbreeding The child is measured for distance from each member of the population and culled if an overly close relative is found. This method of *incest prevention* [22] reduces the likelihood of inbreeding that may otherwise flood the population with similar games, reducing the potential for genetic diversity.

Uncertainty and surprise—two key aspects of game play—are just as important in game design, as players want new and interesting challenges.

Note that since child rule sets are not optimised, then the presence of introns will exaggerate the measured distance between games whose working code is otherwise equivalent. This is not of major concern, however, as such introns still represent differentiated genetic material that may contribute differently to future generations.

Aesthetic Fitness The child game has now survived all critical tests, and is measured for aesthetic fitness using the set of 16 best predictors found in Chap. 4. The aesthetic value returned from the Criticism module will only be approximate as the game's policy is unlikely to be optimal and hence trends in play may not accurately reflect those that would occur between real players. This preliminary estimate will later be superseded by a more accurate measurement if the game proves to be of interest and its policy optimised, but is sufficient for approximately ranking the child within the current population.

An alternative fitness measure called *Pareto scoring* is often used for evolutionary processes, in which individuals are measured component by component, and one individual is said to dominate the other if none of its components are worse than the corresponding components of the other and at least one is better [35]. This means that individuals which improve on any part of the problem are preferred, producing offspring that are likely to improve on the overall problem. Pareto scoring was not used for games, however, as it is more important to measure the rule set as a functioning whole (phenotype) than its individual components (genotype). Note that rule fragility means that individuals with similar genotypes, and hence close in terms of game distance, may differ significantly in value.

Viability Filter While the initial aesthetic measurement may be approximate, it provides enough information to filter out overtly flawed games using a simple but effective viability test. Games that pass this test are marked as "viable" and noted for further investigation:

- *Completion* >0.5: Most games reach a conclusion.
- *Balance* >0.5: No significant advantage to either player.
- *Advantage* <0.5: No significant first move advantage.
- *Duration* <0.5: Games end in a reasonable number of moves.

This viability filter corresponds to the *reference* component of Stiny and Gips' [54] algorithmic aesthetics system and decides whether a rule set constitutes a game that is complete, correct and provides a meaningful contest for its players.

Final Population The final step of the evolutionary process is to insert offspring into the population according to aesthetic fitness. This is a point at which our approach differs from standard GP practice, as no parsimony pressure is applied and *all* children are inserted into the population regardless of quality, hence the population was rife with flawed rules and inferior or even unplayable games. Note, however, that fitter parents were selected more often.

This seems at odds with the general wisdom against the presence of *introns* and *bloat* in the population, but it proved necessary for success in this case. Sanitising the population had the effect of producing offspring that were mostly just slight variations of their original ancestors, as it is highly unlikely that two given rule sets will recombine and mutate to produce superior offspring due to rule fragility. Instead, it proved more effective to flood the population with introns that would act as recessive genes and recombine in unexpected and hopefully serendipitous ways over many generations; this was where true innovation emerged during the experiments. Relaxing parsimony pressure had the effect of reducing the population's average fitness but increasing the amount and variety of working (and non-working) genetic material available.

The evolutionary process repeats until the desired number of games are created, or the time limit runs out. Those games marked as "viable" have their policies optimised and their aesthetic score remeasured; these are the end product of the evolutionary process. Typically 1–2% of non-culled children proved to be viable.

5.3 Experiment III: Game Synthesis

Experiment III was designed to test the effectiveness of the game design process, and whether the aesthetic measurements thus obtained may be used to reliably identify games of interest.

Method The database of 79 source games from Experiment I was used as the initial population and a number of evolutionary runs conducted on three standard Windows machines over one week. Those new games deemed viable which were then ranked by aesthetic fitness and a follow-up survey conducted (similar in format to that of Experiment I) to compare the predicted rankings with human player preferences.

Subjects 27 subjects participated in the follow-up survey, recruited mostly from the 57 participants of Experiment I.

Results Figure 5.7 shows a plot of predicted aesthetic score versus player ranking for the new games. There is a visible linear trend with a correlation of -0.6491 (± 0.577), the relationship being negative as higher scores generally correspond to lower (i.e. better) rankings.

This indicates a significant linear correlation between the aesthetic measurements made by Ludi and human player rankings of the 19 viable games. These results support hypothesis II: *That these fundamental indicators may be harnessed for the directed search for new high quality games*, at least in the search for new combinatorial games as judged by this group of subjects.

Fig. 5.7 Predicted score
versus player ranking of
evolved games

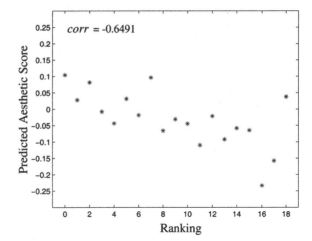

Details of the 19 viable evolved games, and some observations on the dynamics
of the evolutionary process, are presented in Chap. 6. Of particular interest are the
obvious outliers, games #8 and #19, and why might their predicted aesthetic scores
be so much higher than their player rankings would suggest.

Chapter 6
Viable Games

Where the pieces may have different and bizarre motions, with various and variable values, what is only complex is mistaken... for what is profound.

Edgar Allen Poe, *The Murders in the Rue Morgue* (1841)

Abstract The 19 viable rule sets evolved by the Ludi general game system define new combinatorial games that are the culmination of the Ludi project. This chapter describes each of these evolved games and their key characteristics, with particular emphasis on emergent properties and the general success of the evolutionary approach for combinatorial game design. Each description includes a snapshot of the board in its starting position, a summary of the rules and their complete GDL description. The GDL descriptions are shown unoptimised as they emerged from the evolutionary process, complete with optional default nodes fully expanded and erroneous and/or superfluous rules still evident. The games are presented in order of human player preference.

Keywords Ludi · Evolved games · Viable rule sets · Evolutionary game design · Yavalath · Ndengrod/Pentalath · Lammothm

#1. Ndengrod
Computer ranking: #1 (Fig. 6.1).

Move: Add to empty cell, surround capture.
Aim: 5-in-a-row.

Full GDL description:

```
(game Ndengrod
    (players White Black)
    (board (tiling hex) (shape trapezium) (size 7 7))
    (pieces
        (Piece All
            (moves
```

Fig. 6.1 Starting position for
Ndengrod

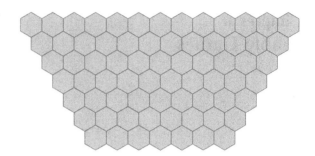

```
        (move (pre (empty to)) (action (push)) (post
            (capture surround))))
      )
    )
  )
  (end (All win (in-a-row 5))))
)
```

Ndengrod, the game ranked most highly by both Ludi and human players, combines Go-like surround capture with a 5-in-a-row goal to good effect. Its quality was not at first recognised (its high ranking was something of a surprise) but subsequent testing has revealed it to be a game of significant depth. Interesting strategies emerge due to its subtle connective basis, as the key to the game appears to lie in the connection of safe groups, which is not immediately obvious.

Figure 6.2 shows a contrived situation by way of example: Black to play. If Black tries to escape along the side with moves **1** and **3** then White can continue pinching this group with moves **2** and **4**. However, fortunes suddenly turn with Black move **5**. White is forced to block an immediate line of five with move **6**, allowing Black to escape with **7**. White will now almost certainly lose the game since Black can capture their isolated piece and complete their line of five at their leisure. This example demonstrates that careful thought is required for even seemingly obvious positions.

It may at first appear that 5-in-a-row is difficult if not impossible to achieve on this medium sized board before it fills up. However, the surround capture mechanism will eventually be exercised and resolve potential deadlocks by clearing cluttered board areas. For example, White may temporarily impede Black with move **6** in the example above, but this piece will inevitably be captured at some point to restore the line threat. Blocks are therefore not permanent and the game has a satisfying self-balancing mechanism.

The combination of surround capture with 5-in-a-row is reminiscent of an existing game Irensei, invented anonymously in 1987 [2]. However, Irensei is somewhat different in character as it requires 7-in-a-row, allows winning suicide moves and is played on a larger square grid on which diagonals count for winning lines but not for surround capture.

Fig. 6.2 Black to play and defend

Ndengrod is one of the two viable games to be commercially published (the other being Yavalath) for which the board shape was changed from a trapezium to a hexagon so that the two games could be published as one set [49]. The name was changed from Ndengrod to Pentalath to highlight the common origins of both games, and also because Ndengrod is simply an ugly name; just like automated game creation, automated name creation did not always succeed.

Yavalath has received the greater acclaim of the two, apparently due to its simpler rules and more immediate play. However, Ndengrod/Pentalath is probably the deepest and most interesting game produced by Ludi, so its #1 ranking by both Ludi and human players is satisfying.

#2. Yavalath

Computer ranking: #4 (Fig. 6.3).

Move: Add to empty cell.
Aim: 4-in-a-row, but lose if 3-in-a-row and not 4-in-a-row.

Full GDL description:

```
(game Yavalath
   (players White Black)
   (board (tiling hex) (shape hex) (size 5))
   (pieces (Piece All (moves (move (pre (empty to))
      (action (push))))))
   (end
      (All win (in-a-row 4))
      (All lose (and (in-a-row 3) (not (in-a-row 4)))))
   )
)
```

Yavalath's end condition (win with 4-in-a-row but lose with 3-in-a-row) is one of the most interesting rule combinations to emerge from the evolutionary process. The concept of 4-in-a-row is immediately familiar to any player, but the lose-with-3 aspect introduces a novel twist that surprises players and allows interesting passages of tactical play due to the resulting possibility of forced moves. A deeper analysis is given in Chap. 7.

Fig. 6.3 Starting position for
Yavalath

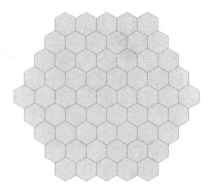

The combination of win with *N*-in-a-row and lose with (*N*-1)-in-a-row constitutes a form of rule tension, with apparently similar rules suddenly becoming incompatible. This allows greater tactical and strategic depth in a game without affecting its clarity (players only need to learn the one basic concept) making this a rather efficient design. Rule tension is a technique used by game designers to add interest to a game, and it is encouraging to see general principles of this sort emerge from the automated process. The fact that 3-in-a-row is infinitely bad while 4-in-a-row is infinitely good had the potential to confuse the simple advisor/policy approach of Ludi's Strategy module, but it proved robust enough to play the game at a reasonable level.

The compound winning condition is one of the most complex to be found in any of the evolved games:

```
(end
    (All win (in-a-row 4))
    (All lose
        (and
            (in-a-row 3)
            (not (in-a-row 4))
        )
    )
)
```

This finely balanced combination required several generations to achieve, of which most of its incarnations involved superfluous or impossible variations as this combination grew in complexity and its parameters became more finely tuned. These flawed variations represent passive genes that allowed the full mechanism to come about, which emphasises the importance of *not* culling superfluous rules during evolution. If such culling were performed then it would be extremely unlikely that this interesting rule combination would have ever evolved spontaneously. In addition, some of Yavalath's ancestors received poor aesthetic scores, and if the population were more aggressively culled to remove unfit individuals during evolution then these crucial steps in its lineage would have been removed.

Fig. 6.4 Starting position for Rhunthil

Yavalath's innovative winning rule did not previously exist for any known game, and it has since gone on to inspire the creation of similar games by human designers (discussed further in Chap. 7). It has proven more popular than Pentalath due to its shorter learning curve and has gone on to become highly ranked on the world's foremost online board game resource [2].

#3. Rhunthil
Computer ranking: #3 (Fig. 6.4).

Move: Add to empty cell, plus several complex movement choices.
Aim: 5-in-a-row.

Full GDL description:

```
(game Rhunthil
  (players White Black)
  (board (tiling square i-nbors) (shape square) (size 8 8))
  (pieces
    (StoneA All
      (label A
        (move (pre (empty to)) (action (push)) (post
          (capture surround)))
        (move (action (push)) (post (capture surround))))
      )
      (moves
        (move (pre (and (empty to) (= (phase to) 1))) (action
          (push)))
        (move
          (pre (and (Piece-state from) (connected)))
          (action (pop) (push))
```

```
                    (post (capture))
                    )
                )
            )
            (StoneB All
              (label B)
              (moves
                (move
                  (pre
                    (and (occupied to) (or (= (phase to)1) (!=
                      (phase to) 2)))
                  )
                    (action (push))
                  )
                )
            )
            (Stone All
              (state 1 //BUG
                (move
                  (pre (empty to))
                  (action) //BUG
                  (post (capture surround))
                )
              )
              (moves
                (move (pre (empty to)) (action (push)))
                (move (action (pop)) (post (inc-state)))
              )
            )
        )
        (start (in-hand(StoneB) 4) (in-hand (StoneA Black) 2))
        (end (All win(in-a-row 5)))
    )
```

Rhunthil's high ranking by both Ludi and human players is something of a mystery. Its rules are verbose, barely comprehensible and include a dangerously malformed piece definition (Stone) that somehow survived the parsing stage; presumably this malformed rule is never triggered in actual play.

This lack of clarity was borne out in the anonymous comments from survey participants who invariably describe the rules as "confusing", with one observing that Rhunthil might be quite interesting to play if only they could wrap their mind around the rules. This intuition appears to have some merit, as borne out in Ludi's self-play analysis, and it seems that human players gave it the benefit of the doubt.

Fig. 6.5 Starting position for
Teiglith

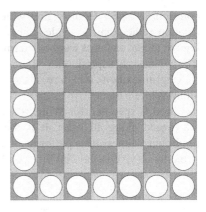

#4. Teiglith
Computer ranking: #7 (Fig. 6.5).

Move: Move to cell connected by friendly pieces, can stack (phase is irrelevant).
Aim: Mover wins if there are no legal moves.

Full GDL description:

```
(game Teiglith
   (players White Black)
   (board (tiling square) (shape square) (size 7))
   (pieces
      (Stone All
         (moves
            (move
            (pre (and (> (group-size to) (phase to))
                 (connected)))
            (action (pop) (push))
            )
          )
        )
      )
   (start (place (Stone White) home))
   (end (All win (no-move)))
)
```

Teiglith is a Nim-like game [7] in which pieces are shared by both players. This
is serendipitous, otherwise Black would have no moves and win on their first turn
since the game starts with only White pieces on the board.

The combination of connected movement with the no-move winning condition
is another example of good emergence, as these rules encourage games to converge elegantly to a solution. Further, this combination of rules instils a group

connection aspect to the game which applies to the many isolated groups that develop rather than a single global group. This concept does not exist for any known game, as far as can be determined. The (> (*group-size to*) (*phase to*)) clause is superfluous.

Teiglith exploits a feature of the Ludi system by specifying that all pieces start along White's home row (*start* (*place* (Stone White) *home*)). Since no direction is specified for White, then a default direction of all is used and pieces are placed along all sides. It is the most viable evolved game in terms of the preliminary fitness tests performed during evolution, and would have been the only game to survive if the viability cutoffs had been raised from 0.5 to 0.7.

#5. Elrostir
Computer ranking: #11 (Fig. 6.6).

Move: Add to empty cell.
Aim: Lose if no move or 3-in-a-row (includes diagonals).

Full GDL description:

```
(game Elrostir
   (players White Black)
   (board (tiling square i-nbors) (shape square) (size 5))
   (pieces (Piece All (moves (move (pre (empty to))
      (action (push)))))))
   (end (All lose (or (no-move) (in-a-row 3)))))
)
```

Elrostir is a simple game featuring the intriguing lose-with-3-in-a-row rule seen in Yavalath. This rule is surprisingly easy to fall victim to on the 8-connected square grid with diagonals—much more so than on Yavalath's 6-connected hexagonal grid—and some concentration is required when playing this game. Elrostir is rather puzzle-like in nature but also quite cold, as there are not many move choices each turn but their potential for disaster my not be immediately obvious. It is ranked more highly by human players than by Ludi, perhaps indicating some

Fig. 6.6 Starting position for Elrostir

Fig. 6.7 Starting position for
Lammothm

degree of surprise that the game holds for human players due to the "fog of war"
that brute force computer analysis cuts through and fails to appreciate.

The "lose if no move" rule is detrimental to the game as the first player will
win if the board has an odd number of cells and both players manage to avoid
forming 3-in-a-row. Indeed, the first move advantage is measured at 0.35 for
Elrostir, which is dangerously high.

Elrostir is the most evolved game of the viable group, being the result of 15
generations of breeding. Its rule combination does not exist for any known game,
as far as can be determined.

Game #6. Lammothm
Computer ranking: #6 (Fig. 6.7).

Move: Add to empty cell, surround capture.
Aim: Connect own regions (includes diagonals).

Full GDL description:

```
(game Lammothm
  (players White Black)
  (board
    (tiling square i-nbors) (shape square) (size 8 8)
    (regions (White n) (White s) (Black e) (Black w))
  )
  (pieces
    (Stone All
      (moves
        (move
          (pre (and (empty to) (or (has-freedom) (cre-
            ates-freedom)))))
```

Fig. 6.8 Starting position for
Gorodrui

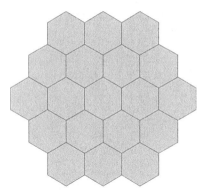

```
(action (push))
(post (capture surround))
  )
 )
 )
 )
(end (All win (connect own-regions)))
)
```

Lammothm is similar to the excellent game Gonnect which grafts a connective goal onto standard Go [2], except that Gonnect allows connection to either pair of opposite sides and does not involve diagonal connection. Lammothm is less interesting as the presence of i-nbors (diagonals) means that groups are harder to surround and therefore capture, and that connection is easier.

Lammothm is a first generation game and hence one of the least evolved viable games. Since Gonnect can be played successfully with a connect-own-sides goal, then Lammothm is only one mutation away (the removal of the i-nbors attribute) so it is disappointing that Ludi did not reinvent Gonnect at some point. This is perhaps a downside of the ad hoc nature of mutation in particular and the evolutionary approach in general.

#7. Gorodrui
Computer ranking: #8 (Fig. 6.8).

Move: Add to empty cell, move to empty cell if distance = state+1, increment state.
Aim: Lose if no move.

Full GDL description:

```
(game Gorodrui
  (players White Black)
  (board (tiling hex) (shape hex) (size 3))
  (pieces
     (Stone All
```

```
(state 1 //BUG: moves element crossed over with a
state element.
  (move (pre (empty from)) (action (push)))
)
(moves
  (move (pre (empty to)) (action (push)))
  (move
    (pre
      (and
        (enemy from) (empty to) (= (+ (piece-
        state) 1) (distance))
      )
    )
    (action (pop) (push))
    (post (inc-state))
  )
)
)
)
(start (in-hand (Stone All) 5))
(end (All lose (no-move)))
)
```

Gorodrui is an interesting puzzle-like game in which each move increments the piece-state and limits that piece's future movement choices, which means that piece movement becomes increasingly constrained and games quickly converge to a conclusion. This mechanism does not exist for any known game, as far as can be determined.

Gorodrui is a first generation game and hence one of the least evolved viable games, but shows the emergence of an interesting new rule combination.

#8. Pelot
Computer ranking: #2 (Fig. 6.9).

Fig. 6.9 Starting position for Pelot

Move: Add to empty cell, move to connected cell whose distance ≠ state, stacking allowed (increment piece-state after moving).
Aim: 4-in-a-row (no diagonals).

Full GDL description:

```
(game Pelot
   (players White Black)
   (board (tiling square) (shape square) (size 5))
   (pieces
      (Stone All
         (moves
            (move (pre (empty to)) (action (push)))
            (move
               (pre (and (owner from) (!= (piece-state)
                  (distance)) (connected)))
               (action (pop) (push))
               (post (inc-state))
            )
         )
      )
   )
   (end (All win (in-a-row 4)))
)
```

Pelot is something of a discrepancy, achieving a high ranking from Ludi but only a mediocre ranking from human players. This may be due to the somewhat mystifying movement rule making good use of the small board in principle, but confuses human players and ruins the clarity of the game so that strategies are hard to formulate. This appears to be a game that is more suited to computers than humans.

#9. Hale
Computer ranking: #15 (Fig. 6.10).

Fig. 6.10 Starting position for Hale

Move: Add to empty cell.
Aim: 4-in-a-row (no diagonals).

Full GDL description:

```
(game Hale
  (players White Black)
  (board (tiling square) (shape square) (size 8 8))
  (pieces (Piece All (moves (move (pre (empty to)) (action
    (push))))))
  (end (All win (in-a-row 4)))
)
```

Hale is a standard 4-in-a-row game except that diagonal lines are not counted. The fact that only orthogonal lines count reduces the chance for threats and hence scope for interesting play, but presumably the novelty value of this minor variant stirred some interest in human players.

#10. Quelon
Computer ranking: #10 (Fig. 6.11).

Move: Add to empty cell.
Aim: Lose if 4-in-a-row (with diagonals).

Full GDL description:

```
(game Quelon
  (players White Black)
  (board (tiling square i-nbors) (shape square) (size 8 8))
  (pieces (Piece All (moves (move (pre (empty to))
    (action (push))))))
  (end (All lose (in-a-row 4)))
)
```

Fig. 6.11 Starting position
for Quelon

Fig. 6.12 Starting position
for Duath

Quelon is a 4-in-a-row game with a twist: a player loses by making 4-in-a-row. This makes it a rather cold game in which players vie for non-losing cells while trying to reduce the opponent's options.

#11. Duath
Computer ranking: #12 (Fig. 6.12).

Move: Add to empty cell.
Aim: Win if 4-in-a-row (with diagonals).

Full GDL description:

```
(game Duath
   (players White Black)
   (board (tiling square i-nbors) (shape square) (size 6))
   (pieces (Piece All (moves (move (pre (empty to)) (action
      (push))))))
   (end (All win (in-a-row 4))))
)
```

Duath is a standard 4-in-a-row game and was lucky not to have been culled as a duplicate. Presumably this was the first 4-in-a-row game on a 6 × 6 board encountered by the system.

#12. Elrog
Computer ranking: #17 (Fig. 6.13).

Move: Add to empty cell.
Aim: 4-in-a-row (with diagonals).

Fig. 6.13 Starting position
for Elrog

Full GDL description:

```
(game Elrog
   (players White Black)
   (board phase (tiling square i-nbors) (shape square)
      (size 6))
   (pieces (Piece All (moves (move (pre (empty to))
      (action (push))))))
   (end (All win (in-a-row 4))))
)
```

Elrog is a standard 4-in-a-row game. The rules contain a vestigial *phase* element, otherwise it would probably have been culled as an inbred duplicate. This suggests that more aggressive culling of vestigial rules may be warranted at the conclusion of the evolutionary process.

#13. Vairilth
Computer ranking: #9 (Fig. 6.14).

Move: Add to empty cell.
Aim: Connect own regions and no move.

Full GDL description:

```
(game Vairilth
   (players White Black)
   (board
      (tiling hex ) (shape rhombus ) (size 7)
      (regions (White ne) (White sw ) (Black se ) (Black nw) )
   )
   (pieces (Piece All (moves (move (pre (empty to))
         (action (push))))))
   (end (All win (and (no-move) (connect own-regions)))))
)
```

Fig. 6.14 Starting position
for Vairilth

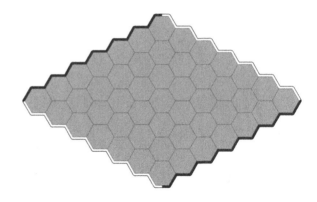

Fig. 6.15 Starting position
for Ninniach

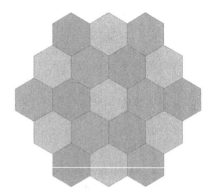

Vairilth is identical to Hex except that games continue until the winning player
has no move, in other words the board becomes full. This superfluous extension of
the game (the outcome cannot change once a winning connection is made) would
appear to be a serious flaw, but could be the very reason that this game survived.
Without it, many games would have been much shorter (Hex games typically only
use a small part of the board) perhaps causing this game to fail the duration aspect
of the viability test. This could be an argument against having a fixed preferred
game length M_{pref} for all games.

#14. Ninniach
Computer ranking: #16 (Fig. 6.15).

Move: Add to an empty cell of your phase, move to a connected cell at least as
high to capture.
Aim: Lose if 4-in-a-row (with diagonals).

Full GDL description:

```
(game Ninniach
   (players White Black)
   (board (tiling hex) (shape hex) (size 3))
   (pieces
      (Stone All
         (moves
            (move
               (pre (and (= (phase to) (mover)) (empty to)))
               (action (push))
            )
            (move
               (pre
                  (and
                     (owner from) (connected) (<= (height from)
                     (height to))
                  )
               )
               (action (pop) (push)) (post (capture))
            )
         )
      )
   )
   (end (All lose (no-move)))
)
```

Ninniach makes good use of the tiny board 3-cells-per-side board by having a rather confusing movement rule and being one of the few games to exploit cell phases. Note that the rule specifying that pieces can only move to connected cells at least as high means that pieces cannot move to empty cells; this is an alternative way to phrase [not (empty to)], an emergent but inefficient rule combination.

#15. Pelagonn
Computer ranking: #13 (Fig. 6.16).

Move: Add to empty cell.
Aim: 5-in-a-row.

Full GDL description:

```
(game Pelagonn
   (players White Black)
   (board (tiling trunc-square) (shape square) (size 8))
```

Fig. 6.16 Starting position
for Pelagonn

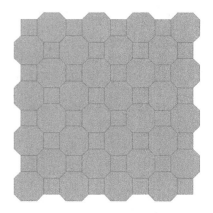

```
(pieces (Piece All (moves (move (pre (empty to))
   (action (push))))))
(end (All win (in-a-row 5)))
)
```

Pelagonn is a standard 5-in-a-row game on an unusual tiling.

#16. Valion
Computer ranking: #14 (Fig. 6.17).

Move: Add to empty cell with at least one enemy neighbour (stacking allowed).
Aim: 3-in-a-row but lose if 4-in-a-row or group (with diagonals).
Full GDL description:

```
(game Valion
  (players White Black)
  (board (tiling square i-nbors) (shape square) (size 4))
  (pieces
    (Stone All
      (moves
        (move (pre (>= (num-nbors to enemy) 1)) (action
          (push)))
        (move (pre (and (empty to) (connected))) (action
          (push)))
      )
    )
  )
  (start (place (Stone White) A1) (place (Stone Black)
    D4))
  (end (All win (in-a-row (All lose (or (in-a-row 4)
    (group))))))
)
```

Fig. 6.17 Starting position
for Valion

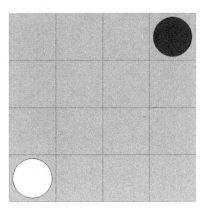

Valion is not a very interesting game due to the small board size, but has two
points of interest:

- The starting placements are a serendipitous combination with the movement
  rules, otherwise neither player would be able to make any moves.
- It contains a variation of the Yavalath "win with four but lose with three" end
  condition.

The second movement rule (add to connected empty cell) is superfluous. Note
that the *group* end condition only applies if there is more than one piece of a given
colour in play.

#17. Eriannon
Computer ranking: #19 (Fig. 6.18).

Move: Add to empty cell.
Aim: 4-in-a-row (no diagonals).

Full GDL description:

```
(game Eriannon
    (players White Black)
    (board (tiling square) (shape square) (size 7))
    (pieces (Piece All (moves (move (pre (empty to)) (action
      (push))))))
    (end (All win (in-a-row 4)))
)
```

Eriannon was by far the game with the lowest evaluation by Ludi. Its rules are
identical to those of Hale (#9) except that it is played on a 7 × 7 board rather than
an 8 × 8 board. This difference in size appears to be critical, making it more
difficult than interesting to achieve 4-in-a-row on the smaller board without
diagonals.

Fig. 6.18 Starting position
for Eriannon

Fig. 6.19 Starting position
for Bregorme

#18. Bregorme
Computer ranking: #18 (Fig. 6.19).

Move: Add to empty cell.
Aim: Connect own regions (with diagonals).

Full GDL description:

```
(game Bregorme
   (players White Black)
   (board
      (tiling square i-nbors) (shape square) (size 8 8)
      (regions (White n) (White s) (Black e ) (Black w))
   )
   (pieces (Piece All (moves (move (pre (empty to))
      (action (push)))))))
   (end (All win (connect own-regions)))
)
```

Fig. 6.20 Shared
connections on the square
grid

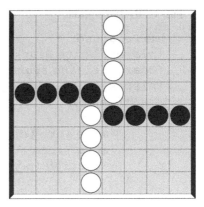

Fig. 6.21 Starting position
for Pelagund

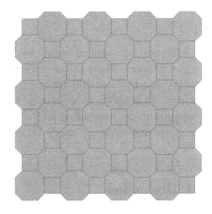

Bregorme is a standard connection game on the square grid, with the presence
of diagonal connections making it a race game as both players can connect across
the same diagonal, making it hard to block connections especially on this relatively
small board size.

Figure 6.20 shows an example in which both players have established a winning path; the first player to complete theirs would have won this game. Connection games on the square grid typically only work if some special mechanisms
is employed to decide diagonal connections for one player or the other.

#19. Pelagund
Computer ranking: #5 (Fig. 6.21).

Move: Add to empty cell or move to connected cell, with stacking.
Aim: 6-in-a-row or no move.

Full GDL description:

```
(game Pelagund
  (players White Black)
  (board (tiling trunc-square) (shape square) (size 8))
  (pieces
    (Stone All
      (moves
        (move (pre (empty to)) (action (push)))
        (move (pre (and (owner from) (connected)))
          (action (pop) (push)))
      )
    )
  )
  (end (All win (in-a-row 6)) (All win (no-move)))
)
```

Pelagund was ranked highly by Ludi (#5) but was the game least preferred by human players. There is no obvious reason for this discrepancy, except perhaps that six in-a-row is a difficult and somewhat tedious challenge that requires a lot of patience to achieve, especially as pieces may stack on connected pieces without constraint to cut impending lines. This is one case in which Ludi saw something in the game that human players did not—or simply misjudged it.

6.1 Discussion

The first thing to note is the general success of the approach: Ludi was able to correlate aesthetic measurements of games with human player rankings with a high degree of accuracy, and hence able to identify those evolved games of most interest. Several of the final 19 games exhibit novel and interesting rule combinations, and those ranked #1 and #2 by human players—Ndengrod and Yavalath— have proven to be of exceptional quality. Yavalath, in particular, features a striking rule mechanism not seen before, hence is an example of Boden's H-Creativity in action [9]. Teiglith (#4), Elrostir (#5), Gorodrui (#7) and Valion (#16) demonstrate the system's usefulness as a creative assistant even with games of average or below average appeal. While not successful as games, each involve interesting rule mechanisms that authors might use as inspiration for future designs.

However, the surprising prevalence of N-in-a-row games in the output was a concern. 63% of the final games (12 out of 19) featured N-in-a-row goals, as opposed to 29% (23 out of 79) in the initial data set. By comparison, the BGG database lists less than 250 N-in-a-row style games [2], making up only around 5% of known abstract games and a much lower percentage of all known board games.

This over-representation may be a reflection of the prevalence of N-in-a-row games in the inspiring set, the superiority of the N-in-a-row advisor over other advisors, or simply indicate that this is a robust rule that thrives in more contexts than others [15]. On the one hand it is interesting to see that innovative games can indeed be derived from Tic Tac Toe, but on the other hand this bias has been seen to mask the true versatility of the system in the public eye. This preference for N-in-a-row games may also be a symptom of the evolutionary process, as this rule is reasonably self-contained and can provide at least a base level of play in combination with almost any other rule, hence is associated with fitter individuals on average.

Evolutionary search is ad hoc in nature and does not perform a systematic coverage of even the local search space. This is highlighted by the fact that the system quickly found Lammothm (#6) but did not then go on to find the far superior Gonnect with the deletion of a single attribute. More systematic alternatives such as Monte Carlo Tree Search (MCTS) [16], Self-Adaptive Greedy Estimate (SAGE) [30] or the use of *metaheuristics* such as Iterated Local Search (ILS) [37] might have more success in optimising games within their local region of the search space. This will become increasingly important for fine-tuning games to find the optimal board size, starting configuration, and so on, for a given rule set.

Similarly, some drawbacks with the evolutionary approach became evident with the need to retain introns as dormant genetic material and relax parsimony pressure so that all offspring were kept regardless of fitness. Both aspects were found to be necessary for interesting results to emerge, but both point to inefficient search that more systematic methods might address.

Chapter 7
Yavalath

> *The best games are not those in which all goes smoothly and steadily toward a certain conclusion, but those in which the outcome is always in doubt.*
>
> George B. Leonard

Abstract Yavalath is the most successful game evolved by the Ludi general game system. This chapter gives a complete description of the rules and analyses the forcing move mechanism that makes Yavalath so interesting. Some strong patterns and tactical tips are given, in addition to the solution of a puzzle and other aspects such as the first move advantage, draws and adding a third player. The publication of Yavalath and its reception by game players and designers is briefly discussed, as well as its general acceptance among the board game community and its possible role as an inspiration for subsequent games.

Keywords Yavalath · Forcing move · First move advantage · Swap rule · Three-player game · BoardGameGeek

7.1 Analysis

The simplicity of Yavalath's rules belie a tactical depth due to the potential for sequences of forcing moves. This section explores this forced move mechanism, including its use to solve the puzzle proposed in Chap. 1 and its prevalence in a number of strong patterns. It is demonstrated that the opening player has a strong (winning) advantage unless an additional rule is used to balance the game.

7.1.1 Rules

Yavalath is played on a hexagonal field of hexagons which is initially empty. The standard board size is five cells per side (Fig. 7.1).

Two players, White and Black, take turns adding a piece of their colour to an empty cell. A player wins by making 4-in-a-row of their colour (or more) but loses

Fig. 7.1 The Yavalath board

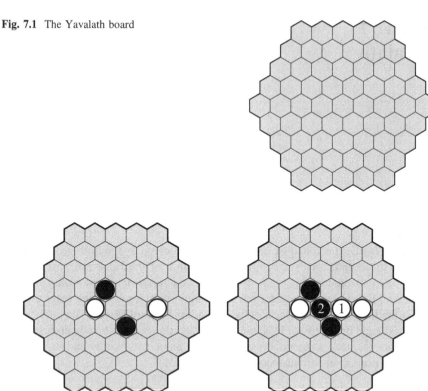

Fig. 7.2 A forcing move by White

by making 3-in-a-row of their colour without also making 4-in-a-row (or more). If the board fills without either player winning or losing, then the game is a draw.

Swap Rule: White makes the first move, then Black has the choice of either swapping colours—effectively stealing the first move—or continuing with their move as usual. This discourages White from making an overly strong opening move near the board centre.

7.1.2 Forcing Moves

The key tactical play in Yavalath is the *forcing move*, as shown in Fig. 7.2. White move **1** threatens to make a line of four white pieces next turn, hence Black is forced to play blocking move **2** to intervene. Unfortunately for Black, this forced blocking move completes a line of three black pieces to lose the game.

Games are typically won using sequences of such forcing moves to manipulate the opponent into disadvantageous and ultimately losing positions. Long sequences of forcing moves can be difficult to predict correctly, especially if forced replies by the opponent themselves trigger further forced replies from the mover,

Fig. 7.3 White to play and
win

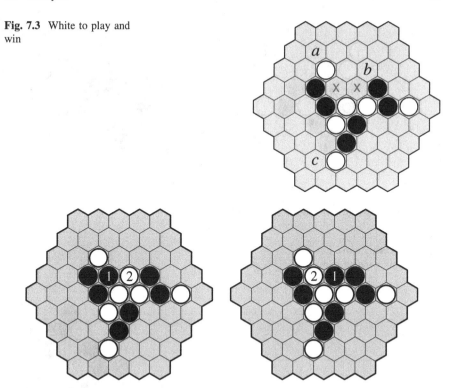

Fig. 7.4 Black can force a win with either move X

and so on. Players can therefore plan ahead with some degree of certainty, but
must be careful of surprises that might lie in wait once a forced exchange is
triggered.

7.1.3 Puzzle Solution

With this in mind, consider the simple puzzle presented in Chap. 1, with White to
play and win (Fig. 7.3). A Black move **1** at either cell X will force a losing reply **2**
from White, as shown in Fig. 7.4. Hence Black must not be allowed to make either
of these moves, and the only way to achieve this is for White to go on the offensive
with forcing moves of their own.

White has three forcing moves available to them, marked *a*, *b* and *c* in Fig. 7.3.
A move **1** at either *a* or *b* would force a reply **2** from Black as shown in Fig. 7.5,
but each of these replies would in turn force a losing reply **3** from White. Such
forcing moves that come back to hurt the mover are called *rebounds* (similar but
opposite to the Go concept of "snap-backs").

The only non-losing choice available to White is therefore move **1** at
c (Fig. 7.6). This forces a harmless reply **2** from Black and sets White up for move

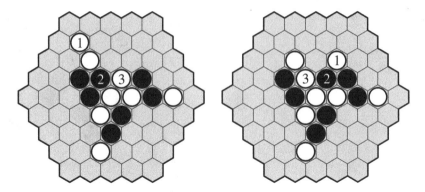

Fig. 7.5 Forcing moves *a* and *b* lose for White

Fig. 7.6 Forcing move *c* is
White's only winning play

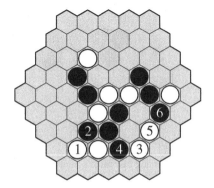

3, which forces another harmless reply **4**. White can then play move **5** which
forces the losing reply **6** from Black.

7.1.4 Strong Patterns

Triangular piece formations tend to be strong. For example, the small size-2
triangle shown in Fig. 7.7 allows White to launch a variety of winning attacks.

Figures 7.8 and 7.9 show forced winning sequences by White both above the
triangle's apex (7.8) and below its base (7.9). Both of these attacks can be applied
in each of three rotations and two reflections, hence it is difficult to block all
possible attacks from all three sides of the small triangle. Players must therefore be
wary of the opponent forming such patterns unless suitable precautions are taken.

Medium size-3 and large size-4 triangles (Figs. 7.10, 7.11) are also strong
formations that allow forced wins, as shown. However, medium and large triangles
are easier to block—it is usually sufficient to block one side—and hence do not
present as much danger as small triangles.

Fig. 7.7 The small size-2
triangle is a strong pattern

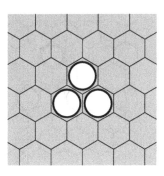

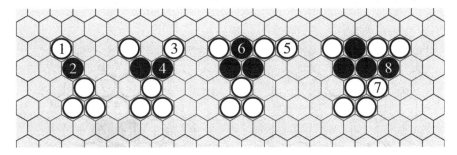

Fig. 7.8 White can force a win above the apex...

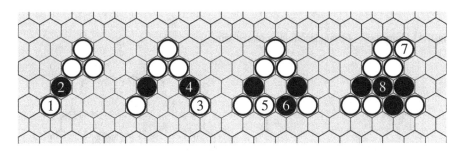

Fig. 7.9 ...and can force a win below the base

7.1.5 First Move Advantage

White has a huge (winning) advantage if allowed an unconstrained opening move. Figure 7.12 shows how White can form a small triangle with their first three moves, which Black is helpless to defend against. This strong opening was first pointed out by Nestor Romeral Andrès in 2011.

Figure 7.13 shows how it is possible to block a small triangle on all three sides with only three pieces. However, White can choose which way to orient the triangle with their third piece to avoid this situation, so Black would have to catch White napping to achieve such a blockade.

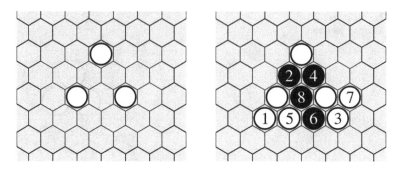

Fig. 7.10 Medium size-3 triangles allow a forced win

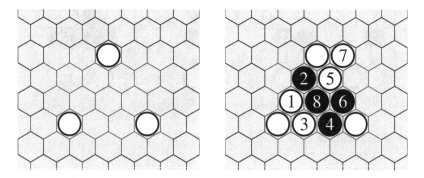

Fig. 7.11 Large size-4 triangles allow a forced win

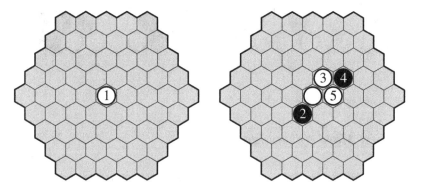

Fig. 7.12 A strong (winning) opening for White

The solution to this imbalance is the *swap rule*, which enables Black to swap colours in lieu of making their first move, to discourage White from making an overly strong opening move. This rule is used to successfully balance openings in a number of combinatorial games.

Fig. 7.13 Black foils White

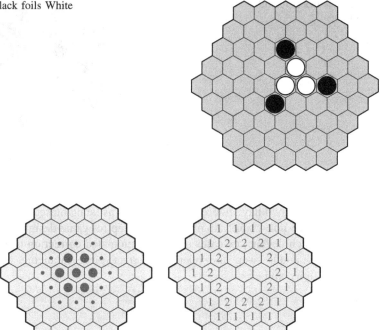

Fig. 7.14 Openings to swap (*left*) and openings to make (*right*)

Figure 7.14 (left) shows opening moves that Black should swap. The large dots represent moves that should undoubtedly be swapped, while the small dots represent moves that appear to be reasonably balanced. Opening moves in unmarked cells need not be swapped as their proximity to the board edge reduces the danger of the small triangle on that side. A general rule of thumb is: *swap any opening move that is three or more cells away from the board edge.*

Figure 7.14 (right) shows the best opening moves for White. Opening moves along the board edge are too weak to consider, while opening moves one cell away from the edge (marked "1") are weak but plausible. Opening moves two cells away from the edge (marked "2") are stronger and reasonably balanced; the opponent will not necessarily swap such a move.

Ludi did not discover the killer opening described above. It seems obvious in hindsight, but then again nor did any human player discover it until years and hundreds—possibly thousands—of games later. Its detection by exhaustive search would require a search depth of 13 involving over 10^{18} moves, and its detection by tactical analysis (centre → size-2 triangle → forced sequence) is beyond the capabilities of Ludi's simple advisor/policy AI model.

It has always been assumed that Yavalath suffered some degree of first move advantage so the swap rule has been used since its release, but the degree of this advantage has not been fully realised until now. This is possibly just as well,

Fig. 7.15 A indecisive fill
pattern

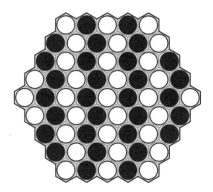

otherwise Ludi would have filtered out its rule set as being biased towards the first
player and hence non-viable. An obvious next step for game design systems is the
detection of such degenerate cases and their automated correction using remedial
measures such as the swap rule, opening contract, piece balancing, initial movement restrictions, and so on.

7.1.6 Draws

Draws, although possible, are extremely rare. Players tend to make a fatal mistake
due to the difficulty of correctly predicting forced sequences, or are forced into
making a losing move as the number of available move choices dwindles in the
end game.

Figure 7.15 shows a possible fill pattern that precludes a result, but which will
not occur in actual play unless both players conspire for a draw.

7.1.7 Three Players

Yavalath works well as a three-player game. The standard two-player rules apply
as specified by Ludi, with the following additions:

(a) Any player to make 3-in-a-row leaves the game (but their pieces remain).
(b) The mover must block the next player if possible.

Rule (a) allows the game to continue when a player loses but a winner is not yet
decided between the remaining two players. Rule (b) removes a potential *kingmaker effect*, which is the undesirable ability of a losing player to decide the
outcome of a game [52]. The move order is: White, Black, Grey.

For example, Fig. 7.16 shows a three-player game with Grey to move. Grey
must move at *a* to block White, then White *must* move at *b* to block Black and

Fig. 7.16 Grey must block
White at *a*

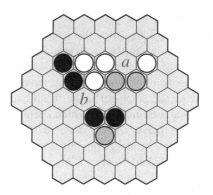

hence lose the game. If rule (b) were not in effect, then Grey would be free to choose between a White loss (or a Black win) with move *a* or a White win with any other move, and the game would hence be decided by social factors rather than strategy. Example by Stephen Tavener.

The three-player version was devised as a natural extension of the two-player game shortly after its invention in 2007.

7.2 Impact

The rest of this chapter deals with the publication of Yavalath, its reception and impact on the broader game playing and game design communities.

7.2.1 Publication

Yavalath was invented by Ludi in November 2007 and published by Nestorgames in July 2009. No secret was made of the fact that this was the first computer-invented board game to be commercially published; this was in fact prominently stated as a marketing point. Yavalath was released in a twin pack with another Ludi game, Ndengrod, which was renamed as Pentalath and translated to the hexagonal Yavalath board for the occasion.

7.2.2 Reception

Yavalath has proven popular with new players as its rules are immediately accessible but their implications are not, making it quite addictive. One of the survey participants admitted to playing Yavalath repeatedly for over an hour, initially to beat the computer opponent but eventually to simply explore the game.

When new players are introduced to the game, there tends to be an "aha!" moment when they discover that forcing moves can make the opponent waste a turn, then shortly afterwards another "aha!" moment when they discover that these forcing moves can also be used to make the opponent play where they may not want to play. These forcing moves appear to be the key to the game, and once a sequence is triggered the result can be something of a surprise (unless the player has a good memory) which keeps the game interesting. There is also the aspect of better players being able to chunk forced sequences into conceptual units to facilitate strategic planning.

Publisher Nestor Romeral Andrès observes that Yavalath works well in attracting casual gamers at conventions and exhibitions due to its simple rules and addictive play. Casual gamers do not appear overly interested in the fact that the game is computer-generated, except to say that they would have expected such a game to be more complex and difficult to play. Hard-core gamers, on the other hand, tend to be very interested in the background of Yavalath, and are surprised that a computer can design such a "fun" game. There does not appear to be much concern within the game-playing community how a game is invented, provided that the game is good.

Game designers have also been surprisingly tolerant of the appearance of Yavalath and its ilk, most choosing to show interest in Ludi's potential as a collaborative tool rather than seeing it as a threat to their creative process (although this may change as automated game designers become more ambitious). Several have even stated that they find the creation of the game names as intriguing as the creation of the games themselves(!) There have been negative comments from designers who see in such automated systems not so much a threat but a challenge that must be risen to, but even in this sense Ludi could be said to inspire creativity in others.

7.2.3 Acceptance

BoardGameGeek (BGG) is a public web site that hosts an online database of almost all known board games (over 52,000) including descriptions, rules, reviews, classifications and player rankings from an international community of over 250,000 users [2]. BGG rankings generally provide a reliable indication of a game's quality, as the voting mechanism—unusually for social networking sites—is hidden such that casual users are unlikely to vote and most scores will therefore be informed decisions from educated users.

Yavalath was ranked #99 in the "Abstract Games" category out of 4,365 entries at the time of writing (August 2011). To put this in perspective, this places Yavalath in the top 2.5% of all abstract board games ever invented (as judged by BGG users) and above the following well-known titles:

- Backgammon (#112)
- Othello (#267)
- Halma (#426)
- Mastermind (#539)
- Chinese Checkers (#546)
- Checkers (#553)

This does not mean that Yavalath is as popular as any of these games (even remotely) but that those players who have tried Yavalath rate it on average more highly than those other games are rated by players who have tried them.

7.2.4 Inspiration

Yavalath's innovative "win with N but lose with $(N-1)$" mechanism has directly inspired the creation of related games by other designers, including Tritt, Cross, Tailath, Morro, Coffee and Epsilon. Some of these games have also been released by Nestorgames.

The Yavalath mechanism has been mapped to other rule contexts. For example, it has been placed in a connective context for Cross: *players win by connecting three non-adjacent sides with a chain of their pieces but lose by connecting two opposite sides beforehand.* Instead of winning with a line of N and losing with a line of N-1, players win with a 3-connection and lose with a 2-connection. This distinction between major and minor connections is reminiscent of the earlier game Unlur, but in this case both players share the same competing objectives and no extended opening contract is needed; Cross is a child of Yavalath.

In at least one known case Yavalath has inspired a designer not to invent a new game but to revisit a related idea, based on group size, that had been shelved years ago and forgotten. Yavalath could be said to have indirectly stimulated creativity by nudging this designer's memory and bringing this idea back into play for further development. It is interesting to note the surprising number of group size games that have emerged in the couple of years since then—more than the total number that had previously existed. Perhaps Ludi has served a wider role as a creative catalyst.

Chapter 8
Conclusion

What you see on the board is only the outcrop of a much larger
world, like mountain peaks above the mist.

Ian Watson, *Queenmagic, Kingmagic*

Abstract The Ludi general game system was designed to interpret, play and
create new combinatorial games using an evolutionary approach, in order to
explore questions of automated game design. This chapter looks back over the
Ludi project, where it succeeded and where it failed, and examines the evidence
for computational creativity afforded by the automated generation of games such
as Yavalath and its siblings. Some possible shortcomings of the evolutionary
process for game design are highlighted.

Keywords Procedural content generation · Computational creativity · Automated
game design · Evolutionary process · Ludi · Yavalath · Lammothm

8.1 Regarding the Hypotheses

This project demonstrated general success in the automated design of combinatorial games. Ludi, in creating new games that human players found interesting,
served to answer the initial hypotheses: it appears that there *do* exist fundamental
(and measurable) indicators of game quality and that these indicators *can* be
harnessed for the directed search for new high quality games. Many aesthetic
criteria were implemented but these should not be considered a complete or
canonical set of indicators for all games; they were a sufficient set for the survey
participants for those games within Ludi's scope.

8.2 Regarding the New Games

Of the 19 new games created by Ludi, two (Ndengrod and Yavalath) proved to be
of exceptional quality and have since been published. Three or four others featured
interesting or innovative rule combinations that might be developed into good

C. Browne, *Evolutionary Game Design*, SpringerBriefs in Computer Science,
DOI: 10.1007/978-1-4471-2179-4_8, © Cameron Browne 2011

games, while the remainder were forgettable. 1,389 legal rule sets were evolved from the inspiring set of 79 games, giving an approximate success rate of 1 viable game per 73 children and 1 exceptional game per 694 children.

Ludi did not exactly reinvent any known game, which is not surprising given its anti-incest mechanism which culled any child that duplicated a member of the population (Ludi would only be able to exactly reinvent games that it did not know). However, it came close. Ndengrod (#1) was not far away from the existing game Irensei and Lammothm (#6) was tantalisingly close to reinventing Gonnect, one of the very best connection games. The removal of a single attribute (*i-nbors*) would have turned Lammothm from a mediocre game into a truly brilliant one.

N-in-a-row games were strongly over-represented in the evolved set for a somewhat disappointing lack of variety; 63% featured *N*-in-a-row goals when only around 5% could be expected in a random selection of board games. While some novel rule combinations did emerge to surprise players, many of the evolved games were essentially clones of each other with only trivial differences. A method for comparing game distance by phenotype (i.e. strategic difference) rather than by genotype (i.e. rule difference) might help address this issue.

8.3 Regarding the Evolutionary Approach

The description of games as Lisp-style S-expressions made them ideal for genetic programming (GP) manipulation. This did indeed prove successful in the creation of interesting games; however, some possible shortcomings of the evolutionary approach became apparent, at least as it was implemented for this project.

Firstly, the search seemed rather inefficient. A large number of valid children had to be generated for each successful game—the number of invalid rule sets culled before measurement was not even counted—which can be problematic when the evaluation of individuals is so time consuming (several hours per game in extreme cases). Secondly, the search seemed rather uncontrolled and something of a lottery. This was possibly exacerbated by the need to flood the population with introns and retain all offspring, hence reducing the search focus.

For example, Lammothm (#6) occurred early in the search requiring only one particular mutation to transform it from a mediocre game to a truly excellent one, but that mutation never occurred and there is no guarantee that it ever would. One can only guess at the number of inferior rule sets rejected by the viability filter which could have been transformed into superior individuals with similarly simple operations.

More systematic (but still randomised) search methods such as Monte Carlo Tree Search (MCTS), Self-Adaptive Greedy Estimate (SAGE) or the use of metaheuristics such as Iterated Local Search (ILS) might provide viable alternatives that could be especially useful for optimising games within their local search regions. These directions are ripe for future research.

8.4 Regarding Computational Creativity

There appears to be evidence of creativity in the operation of Ludi and the invention of Yavalath in particular. Returning to Ritchie's criteria for attributing creativity [47], the system satisfies the following requirements:

- *Novelty*: Yavalath features an interesting rule mechanism not seen before in any previous board game, and several of the lesser games produced by Ludi also feature new, interesting mechanisms. These are examples of Boden's H-Creativity [9].
- *Quality*: Yavalath has been commercially published and is generally well received by new players. It has ranked #99 on the BoardGameGeek database, placing it among the top 2.5% of all known abstract games. Ndengrod also appears to be an excellent game.
- *Typicality*: Yavalath falls squarely within the N-in-a-row family of games, but also subverts this genre with its self-contradictory "win with N but lose with $(N-1)$" rule pairing.
- *Reinvention*: Two of the 19 games produced by Ludi were *almost* reinventions of known games, including one of excellent quality (Gonnect). These are *almost* examples of Boden's P-Creativity [9].

Yavalath has itself inspired creativity in human designers, both directly through its novel rule mechanism and indirectly through association. Ludi can also be said to have indirectly stimulated creativity in designers, by provoking them to produce better games.

It can argued that Yavalath's particular rule combination is obvious and would eventually have been found by someone. However, the fact remains that nobody actually *did* propose this rule combination until Ludi, even though the N-in-a-row region of the search space has been explored by many designers over the years. Evidently there are still gems hiding in even the most well-trodden parts of the combinatorial design space, highlighting the value of systematic localised search in key areas. Computers can focus on such tasks with greater persistence and concentration than human designers, and could yield significant rewards.

Humans can create new rules, while machines can create new combinations of these to maximise their use. The fact that a computer programme cannot act beyond its knowledge of the current domain is one advantage that human designers have over machines. As Countess Lovelace [36] stated:

The Analytical Engine has no pretensions to originate anything.
It can do [only] whatever we know how to order it to perform.

However, I would argue that the evidence presented in this book points to computational creativity in the production of interesting rule combinations, if not in the design of the rules themselves. This potential for higher-level combinatorial creativity is limited by the scope of the rules provided to the system, and is perhaps masked by the programmer's creativity that goes into defining these rules in the first place. Defining games using lower-level atomic rule descriptions instead would allow a more transparent process in which any emergent creativity could not be attributed to the programmer. For example, it would be satisfying if such a system could devise a Go-style surround capture rule, starting with no knowledge beyond the relationships between the pieces and cells on the board. In the meantime, Ludi has demonstrated creativity in the higher-level assembly of known rules.

As to the question of whether the mantle of *creator* should rest with the programme or the programmer, this is still a difficult question. I, as programmer, made the conditions possible for Yavalath to emerge, but Ludi was the tool that found the relevant rule combination and recognised it as a worthwhile game. While I must assume some of the creative responsibility for defining the candidate rules in the first place, the system performed a creative act to produce a high quality artefact that might otherwise never have existed. One of us invented Yavalath, and it wasn't me.

Appendix A
Ludi GDL: Grammar

This appendix presents a formal specification of the complete Game Description Language (GDL) implemented for Ludi. For more detailed descriptions of the structure and component elements see Appendix B (Ludi GDL: Functional Description) or Browne [14].

The symbol ⇒ matches a declaration (LHS) with its definition (RHS).

A.1 Syntax

Definitions	
UPPERCASE	⇒ Symbol types.
lowercase	⇒ Rule clause (ludeme) defined by the language.
Capitalised	⇒ Data type.
italicised	⇒ Keyword, operator, function or built-in clause identifier.
Italicised Cap.	⇒ Player identifier or name.
[item]	⇒ Optional item.
I	⇒ Choice (disjunction).
{a I b I c ...}	⇒ Exactly one of the listed items.
(clause)	⇒ Rule clause (ludeme) bracketed for scoping purposes.
%n	⇒ Variable item to be instantiated as the nth argument.
Symbol Types	
INT	⇒ Signed integer.
UINT	⇒ Unsigned integer.
FLOAT	⇒ Floating point number.
NUMBER	⇒ INT I UINT I FLOAT
BOOL	⇒ { 0 I 1 }
CHAR	⇒ ASCII character in the range 32..128 (not space).
STRING	⇒ CHARs

(continued)

C. Browne, *Evolutionary Game Design*, SpringerBriefs in Computer Science,
DOI: 10.1007/978-1-4471-2179-4, © Cameron Browne 2011

(continued)

Symbol Types	
NAME	$\Rightarrow$ STRING
ITEM	$\Rightarrow$ NUMBER I BOOL I FLAGS I STRING
Plurals	
items	$\Rightarrow$ item [items]
CHARs	$\Rightarrow$ CHAR [CHARs]

A.2 Data Types

PlayerType	$\Rightarrow$ *White* I *Black* I *Grey* I *Red* I *Green* I *Blue* I *Cyan* I *Magenta* I *All* I *None* I *Neutral* I *Current* I *Friend* I *Enemy* I NAME
PlayerState	$\Rightarrow$ *active* I *resigned*
CompassDirn	$\Rightarrow$ *n* I *s* I *e* I *w* I *ne* I *se* I *nw* I *sw*
TurtleDirn	$\Rightarrow$ *f* I *b* I *l* I *r*
PieceType	$\Rightarrow$ NAME I *any* I *current* I *captured*
PieceRecord	$\Rightarrow$ (PieceType [PlayerType] [(*state* UINT)] [(*flags* UINT)] [(*value* INT)])
MoveRecord	$\Rightarrow$ (PieceType MoveType [PlayerType])
Direction	$\Rightarrow$ CompassDirn I TurtleDirn I *any* I *all* I *d-nbors* I *i-nbors* I *current* I *flagged* I *opposite*
Step	$\Rightarrow$ Direction I (Direction {UINT I *line* I *line-of-sight*})
TilingType	$\Rightarrow$ *hex* I *square* I *tri* I *trunc-square*
ShapeType	$\Rightarrow$ *hex* I *square* I *tri* I *rhombus* I *trapezium* I *boardless* I *rot-square*
CoordLabel	$\Rightarrow$ CHAR UINT
CoordType	$\Rightarrow$ CoordLabel I UINT I *from* I *to* I *current* I (CoordType Steps)
CoordRecord	$\Rightarrow$ (CoordType PlayerType State [UINT])
RegionType	$\Rightarrow$ Direction I (CompassDirection UINT) I CoordType I *home* I (*home* UINT) I *away* I (*away* UINT) I (*dirn* UINT) I *all-sides* I *alternating-sides*
RegionSet	$\Rightarrow$ { UINTs I *own-regions* I *all-sides* I *opposite-sides* I *alternating-sides* I (*n-of* {UINT I *half* I *majority*} UINTs) }
RegionRecord	$\Rightarrow$ (PlayerType {RegionType I RegionSet})
CaptureType	$\Rightarrow$ *replace* I *jump* I *surround* I *nbors* I *d-nbors* I *i-nbors* I *edges* I *cells* I *connected* I *swap* I *mimic* I *cap* I *any* I *all* I *this*
ResultType	$\Rightarrow$ *win* I *lose* I *draw*
Tree$<$x$>$	$\Rightarrow$ (x I (*and* Tree$<$x$>$) I (*or* Tree$<$x$>$) I (*not* Tree$<$x$>$) I (*if* x Tree$<$y$>$ Tree$<$z$>$) I (*n-of* {UINT I *half* I *majority*} Tree$<$x$>$))

A.3 Functions

---

bool_function ⇒ {

               BOOL | (*not* BOOL) | (*and* BOOL BOOLs) |

               (*or* BOOL BOOLs) | (*xor* BOOL BOOLs) |

               (= INT INTs) | (!= INT INT) | (< INT INT) |

               (<= INT INT) | (> INT INT) | (>= INT INT) |

               (*empty* CoordType) | (*occupied* CoordType) |

               (*owner* CoordType [PlayerType]) |

               (*enemy* CoordType [PlayerType]) |

               (*friend* CoordType [PlayerType]) |

               (*neutral* CoordType) | (*steps* TurtleDirns) |

               (*adjacent* [*i-nbors*] [*d-nbors*]) |

               (*connected* [PlayerType]) |

               (*in-region* CoordType RegionSet) |

               (*line* [PlayerType] [(*dirn* Direction)] [*i-nbors*]

               [*d-nbors*]) |

               (*contains* CoordType PieceRecord [UINT]) |

               (*has-freedom*) | (*creates-freedom*)

        } ⇒ returns BOOL

int_function   ⇒ {

               INT | (+ INT INTs) | (- INT INT) | (* INT INTs) |

               (/ INT INT) | (% INT INT) | *from* | *to* | *current* |

               (*max* INT INTs) | (*min* INT INTs) |

               (*from* Directions) | (*to* Directions) |

               (*owner* CoordType) | (*height* CoordType) |

               (*num-pieces* CoordType {PlayerType | PieceRecord}) | (*num-edges* CoordType

               State) |

               (*num-nbors* CoordType PlayerType) | (*distance*) |

               (*num-moves*) | (*piece-state* [CoordType]) |

               (*dist-to* UINTs) | (*phase* CoordType) | (*mover*) |

               (*num-flags* [PieceRecord]) | (*state* CoordType) |

               (*if* bool_function [int_function [int_function]]) |

               (*total-cells*) | (*board-width*) | (*board-height*) |

               (*min-dim*) | (*max-dim*) | (*group-size* CoordType) |

               (*nbors* CoordType [int_function]) |

               (*line* [int_function]) | (*capture-num*) |

               (*capture-value*) | (*num-between* PlayerType) |

               (*row* CoordType) | (*col* CoordType)

        } ⇒ returns INT

A.4 Grammar

Game Definition	
game	⇒ (*game* NAME [ITEMs] players equipment rules [support])
rules	⇒ { [pieces] [start] [play] end }
Players	
players	⇒ (*players* {NAME	(NAME CompassDirection)}s)
Equipment	
equipment	⇒ { board } // only board games supported
board	⇒ (*board* [*phase*]
	(*tiling* TilingType [*i-nbors*])
	(*shape* ShapeType)
	(*size* UINTs)
	[(*regions* RegionRecords)]
	[NAME]
	)
Pieces and Movement	
pieces	⇒ (*pieces* piece_defns [NAME])
piece_defn	⇒ (NAME
	PlayerType [(*label* STRING)]
	[(*value* INT)] [(*state* State)] [(*flags* Flags)]
	(*moves* move_defns)
	)
move_defn	⇒ (*move*
	[(*priority* UINT)] [*mandatory*]
	[(*label* STRING)]
	[(*dirn* Direction)]
	[(*owner* PlayerType)]
	[(*pre* bool_function)]
	(*action* {*pass* | action_defns})
	[(*post* post_conditions)]
	)
action_defn	⇒ {
	(*pop* [CoordType] [UINT	*all*])	
	(*push* [CoordType] [UINT] [PlayerType] [*trail*])
	}
post_condition	⇒ {
	(*capture* CaptureTypes [PieceRecord] [*optional*] [(*if* fn)])	
	(*convert*
	{
	[PlayerType] State	
	CaptureTypes [PieceRecord] [PlayerType] State
	} [*optional*] [(*if* fn)])	
	(*rotate* {INT	*any*} [*optional*] [(*if* fn)])	
	(*change-dirn* Direction)	

(continued)

(continued)

Game Definition	
	(*displace* Direction [PieceRecord] [UINT]
	[*optional*] [(*if* fn)]) |
	(*cell-state* CoordType [PlayerType] State
	[*optional*] [(*if* fn)]) |
	(*piece-state* [CoordType] [PlayerType] INT
	[*optional*] [(*if* fn)]) |
	(*inc-state* [CoordType] [PlayerType]
	[(*amount* INT)] [(*mod* UINT)]
	[*optional*] [(*if* fn)]) |
	(*add-flags* [CoordType] Flags [*optional*] [(*if* fn)]) |
	(*remove-flags* [CoordType] Flags
	[*optional*] [(*if* fn)]) |
	(*score* int_function [(*if* fn)])
	}

Start Conditions	
start	⇒ (*start* [place_clauses]s [in_hand_clauses]s)
place_clause	⇒ (*place*
	PieceRecord [UINT] [(*phase* UINT)]
	{
	home | (*home* UINTs) |
	CompassDirn | (CompassDirn UINTs) | (*region* UINTs) |
	(*site* UINTs) | CoordLabel | *opposed*
	}s
	)
in_hand_clause	⇒ (*in-hand* PieceRecord UINT)

Play Order	
play	⇒ (*play* [*can-pass*])

End Conditions	
end	⇒ (*end* end_clauses)
end_clause	⇒ (PlayerType ResultType Tree<end_condition>)
end_condition	⇒ {
	(*connect*
	[PieceRecord] [*d-nbors* | *i-nbors* |
	all-nbors] RegionSet [*stack*]
	) |
	(*group* [PieceRecord] [UINT]
	[*d-nbors* | *i-nbors* | *all-nbors*] [*stack*]) |
	(*n-in-a-row* [PieceRecord] UINT
	[*d-nbors* | *i-nbors* | *all-nbors*]) |
	(*pattern* [PieceRecord] Steps) |
	(*reach* [PieceRecord] [UINT| *all*| *fill*] [*stacks*]
	{
	away | (*away* UINT) |
	CompassDirn | (CompassDirn UINT) |
	(*region* UINT) | (*site* UINT) | CoordLabel |

(continued)

(continued)

Game Definition	
	all-sides | (*all-sides* UINT)
	}s
	) |
	(*capture* [PieceRecord] [UINT | *all*]) |
	(*stack* [PieceRecord] UINT [*owner*]) |
	(*state* { CoordRecord | PieceRecord }) |
	(*no-move*)
	}
Support Metadata	
support	⇒ { [advisors] [help] [aim] [ancestry] [rank] [viable] [score] }
advisors	⇒ (*advisors* (NAME FLOAT)s)
help	⇒ (*description* STRINGSs)
aim	⇒ (*aim* STRINGSs)
ancestry	⇒ (*ancestry*
	(*parents* NAME NAME) (*maturity* UINT)
	(*dist* FLOAT FLOAT FLOAT)
	)
rank	⇒ (*ranking* FLOAT)
viable	⇒ (*viable* FLOAT)
score	⇒ (*score* FLOAT [(*old* FLOAT)])

Appendix B
Ludi GDL: Functional Description

This Appendix provides a functional description of the key elements of the Ludi game description language (GDL). A complete formal definition of the grammar is beyond the scope of this paper; for more details see Browne [14].

B.1 Structure

Games are defined as recursive trees of elements of the following form:

(*element* [attributes] [(element ...)s])

The first item of each element is its name which must be unique within its current scope. Each element name must be either a predefined keyword or a user-defined variable, such as a named piece type, that has been previously described within the game's rule set. Italicised symbols indicate keywords, upper case symbols indicate data types, capitalised symbols indicate record types, and square brackets [] denote optional items. Approximately 200 keywords and 20 record types are defined and implemented for the language.

B.2 Game

The root of each rule tree is the main *game* ludeme:

```
game ⇒ (game NAME [params]
          players
          board
          rules
          [support]
       )
```

C. Browne, *Evolutionary Game Design*, SpringerBriefs in Computer Science,
DOI: 10.1007/978-1-4471-2179-4, © Cameron Browne 2011

```
rules ⇒ { [pieces] [start] [play] end }
```

These main ludeme types are now briefly described.

B.3 Players

Player names and directions (mandatory).

```
players ⇒ (players
             {NAME | (NAME CompassDirection)}s
          )
```

Each player has a unique name and is optionally associated with a compass direction indicating direction of play. All games in this study involved two players "White" and "Black".

B.4 Board

Board topology and size (mandatory).

```
board ⇒ (board [phase]
             (tiling TilingType [i-nbors])
             (shape ShapeType)
             (size UINTs)
             [(regions RegionRecords)]
          )
```

Board cells may be phased to alternate colour with neighbours, such as the light and dark cells of a Chess board. Trivalent tilings require three phase colours, as shown in Fig. 3.2. The following tilings are supported:

- *tri*,
- *square*,
- *hex*,
- *trunc-square* (4.8.8 semiregular tiling).

Adjacency is assumed between orthogonal neighbours, while the optional *i-nbors* flag indicates adjacency between indirect (diagonal) neighbours. The following board shapes are supported:

- *tri*,
- *square*,
- *hex*,
- *rhombus*,
- *trapezium*,
- *boardless*.

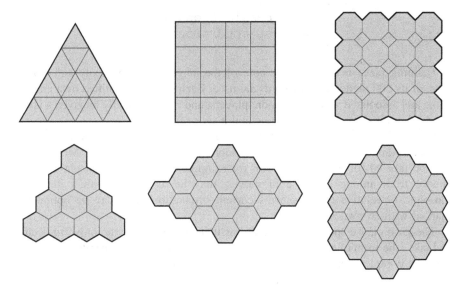

Fig. B.1 Some board types of size 4

The user defines one or more board dimensions depending on tiling and shape, and may optionally define distinct regions of cells for special purposes such as goal areas, promotion zones or connection targets. Figure B.1 shows some examples of supported board types of size 4.

B.5 Pieces and Movement

Piece types and movement rules (optional)

```
     pieces ⇒ (pieces piece_defns [NAME])
piece_defn ⇒ (NAME PlayerType
                [(label STRING)]
                [(value INT)]
                [(state State)]
                (flags Flags)]
                (moves move_defns)
              )
 move_defn ⇒ (move
                [(priority UINT)]
                [mandatory]
                [(label STRING)]
                [(dirn Direction)]
                [(owner PlayerType)]
                [(pre bool_function)]
```

```
(action {pass|actions})
[(post post_conditions)]
)
```

Defining piece behavior is the core of the language's complexity and where most of its 200 predefined keywords are used. Each piece is identified by a unique name and associated with one or more players, and may optionally be given a label for display purposes, a value, a state and a set of flags.

Each piece must have one or more move definitions, optionally marked as mandatory and/or ordered by priority if more than one are provided. Moves may also be labeled for display purposes, for example when the current player must choose from among a choice of moves, may be associated with a direction (absolute or relative to the piece's current orientation) and may be optionally marked with an owner.

The *pre* clause specifies preconditions that must exist for the move to occur, and takes the form of a tree of keywords combined with logical operators that may describe complex conditions. The *action* clause defines the move itself which may involve passing, adding a piece or moving a piece, possibly to stack. The *post* clause specifies postconditions that are exercised after the move, including:

- captures,
- conversions,
- rotations,
- displacement of neighbours,
- piece state updates,
- cell state updates,
- piece flag updates,
- score updates, and so on.

The following example shows how complex move descriptions may be constructed from these simple predicates.

```
(move
   (pre
   (and
      (owner from) (empty to) (line)
      (or
         (not (> (num-between empty) 0))
         (= (num-between enemy) 1)
      )
   )
   (action (pop) (push))
   (post
      (capture (if (>= (height current) 2)) d-nbors)
      (inc-state)
   )
)
```

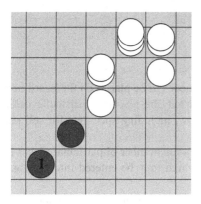 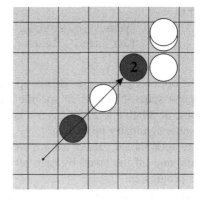

Fig. B.2 A compound move

This movement rule states that the piece may be moved if it belongs to the current player and is moved to an empty board cell along a line that contains either no empty spaces or a single enemy piece (or both). The piece is popped from its current position and pushed to its new position (i.e. it is moved), possibly to stack. Following the move, all orthogonally adjacent stacks of height 2 or more (enemy stacks by default) are captured and the piece's state is incremented. The piece's state may be relevant to another move type for this piece or even other pieces. Figure B.2 shows such a move being executed.

Non-linear move paths, such as knight moves, may be defined in the *pre* clause by relating the move's *to* and *from* cells using a sequence of turtle directions, relative to either the piece's current orientation or a global direction:

- f = forwards,
- b = back,
- l = left,
- r = right.

If no *pieces* ludeme is defined then players add a piece of their colour at an empty cell each turn by default. This is equivalent to the following ludeme, which can be seen in several of the evolved games:

(move (pre (empty to)) (action (push)))

B.6 Start Conditions

Initial board state (optional).

```
start ⇒ (
          [place_clause]s
          [in_hand_clause]s
       )
```

The optional *place_clause*s specify pieces to be placed on the board before the game starts. Numbers of specific pieces may be placed at particular cells or regions, or relative to each player's home row, including specifiers for cell phase and some symmetry operations.

The optional *in_hand_clause*s specify the number of particular pieces held in-hand and off the board by each player, which may be entered into play as the game progresses.

If no *start* ludeme in specified, then the board is initially empty and players hold an infinite number of each piece type in hand.

B.7 Play Order

Constraints on play (optional).

```
play ⇒ ([can-pass])
```

The *play* ludeme specifies whether players may voluntarily pass or not. This was the only constraint on play implemented for the experiments, but other constraints of this type might include first move equaliser, progressive move counts, play order, and so on.

If no *play* ludeme is specified then players may not voluntarily pass. However, they may be forced to pass if they have no valid moves on a given turn, unless the *no-move* end condition is specified.

B.8 End Conditions

Terminating conditions for the game (mandatory).

```
      end ⇒ (end
                  end_clauses
                  [mover-wins|mover-loses|draw]
             )
end_clause ⇒ (PlayerType ResultType
                  Tree<end_condition>
             )
```

The *end* ludeme specifies a number of *end_clause*s and optionally how to handle the case of a move triggering end clauses for both players: *mover-wins*, *mover-loses* or *drawn* game. Each end_clause specifies a player (White, Black or All players), a result type (*win*, *lose* or *draw*) and tree of logical operators relating one or more end conditions of the following types:

- *connect*: Connect two or more target regions of the board, according to optional piece, adjacency and stacking constraints.
- *group*: Form a single connected group of a given size, according to optional piece, adjacency and stacking constraints.
- *in-a-row*: Form a consecutive line of *N* pieces, according to optional piece and adjacency constraints.
- *reach*: Reach the specified goal (cell, region or board side) with the specified number of the specified piece.
- *capture*: Capture the specified number of the specified pieces.
- *eliminate*: Eliminate the specified player.
- *score*: Reach the specified score.
- *stack*: Achieve the specified stack size under certain constraints.
- *state*: Achieve the specified cell or piece state.
- *no-move*: The current player has no moves.

The game ends as soon as any end condition is completely met, and the specified player is awarded the specified result (*win*, *lose* or *draw*).

For example, the following game ends either when White loses by forming a group of size 5 or when either player wins by having no moves and either connecting their sides of the board or forming a stack of height 4:

```
(end
  (White lose (group 5))
    (All win
      (and
      (no-move)
      (or
        (connect own-regions)
        (stack 4)
      )
    )
  )
)
```

B.9 Support Metadata

Specifies additional metadata for the game (optional).

```
support ⇒ {
              [advisors]
              [description]
```

```
            [aim]
            [ancestry]
            [ranking]
            [viable]
            [score]
        }
```

Support items fulfill the following roles:

- advisors: Policy defined by advisors and relative weightings.
- description: Text description of the game for help manual purposes.
- aim: Text description of the aim of the game, which, together with the GGP's tutorial mode, should help new players learn the game quickly.
- ancestry: Information on the game's evolutionary history including its immediate parents, generation number, and average distances from its parents, members of the initial population and members of the final population.
- ranking: Estimated ranking of the game within its population.
- viable: Estimated viability of the game.
- score: Estimated aesthetic score.

The following advisor types are supported:

- *conn*: Connection advisor.
- *group*: Group advisor.
- *nina*: *N*-in-a-row advisor.
- *linecap*: Line cap advisor (enemy cap potential).
- *capt*: Capture advisor (target pieces only).
- *mater*: Material advisor (all pieces).
- *proxe*: Proximity advisor (average distance to enemy pieces).
- *proxm*: Proximity advisor (average distance middle of the board).
- *proxs*: Proximity advisor (average distance to board sides).
- *proxc*: Proximity advisor (average distance to board corners).
- *proxh*: Advancement advisor (average distance from home region).
- *proxg*: Proximity to goal (distance to goal).
- *scor*: Score advisor.
- *state*: State advisor (state existence).
- *stack*: Stack advisor (stack height).
- *mobil*: Mobility advisor (number of legal moves).
- *infl*: Influence advisor (number of reachable empty sites).
- *attack*: Attack advisor (number of reachable enemy sites).
- *defen*: Defence advisor (number of reachable friendly sites).
- *threat*: Threat advisor (number of friendly sites reachable by enemy).

Appendix C
List of Advisors

The following advisors were implemented for Ludi's Strategy module. For further details see Browne [14]:

1. *Proximity to Corners*: Measures the average proximity of pieces to the closest board corner. Encourages players to move towards the corners.
2. *Proximity to Sides*: Measures the average proximity of pieces to the closest board side. Encourages players to move outwards towards the sides.
3. *Proximity to Middle*: Measures the average proximity of pieces to the board centre. Encourages players to move inwards towards the middle of the board (complementary to *Proximity to Middle* but distinct from it).
4. *Proximity to Home*: Measures the average proximity of pieces to their home area. Encourages players to stay near their home area; this may be useful for defending a home area, or may be negated to urge pieces away.
5. *Proximity to Goal*: Measures the distance between pieces and the specified goal. Encourages players to move towards the goal.
6. *Proximity to Enemy*: Measures the average distance between friendly and enemy pieces. Encourages players to surround or otherwise engage with enemy pieces.
7. *Attack*: Measures the value of enemy pieces directly threatened by the mover's pieces. Encourages players to attack enemy pieces.
8. *Defence*: Measures the value of friendly pieces defended by other friendly pieces. Encourages players to defend their own pieces.
9. *Threat*: Measures the value of friendly pieces directly threatened by enemy pieces. Encourages players to avoid threats from enemy pieces.
10. *Material*: Measures the value of pieces on the board. Encourages players to capture enemy pieces, and can also be also useful in non-capture games for encouraging players to add new pieces rather than move existing ones.
11. *Capture*: Measures the value of target pieces on the board. This is distinct from the *Material* advisor as it only counts the target piece(s) specified in the end condition. Encourages players to reduce the number of target pieces.

C. Browne, *Evolutionary Game Design*, SpringerBriefs in Computer Science, DOI: 10.1007/978-1-4471-2179-4, © Cameron Browne 2011

12. *Mobility*: Measures the number of legal moves M available to the player. Encourages players to maximise their movement options.
13. *Influence*: Measures the number of board cells reachable by any move. Encourages players to maximise their movement options.
14. *Score*: Measures the player's score. Encourages players to maximise their score.
15. *State*: Determines whether a specified piece or cell state exists. Encourages players to achieve that state.
16. *Stack*: Measures the player's potential for stack height. Encourages players to build higher stacks where beneficial, and to discourage detrimental stacking behaviour otherwise.
17. *N-in-a-Row*: Measures the player's potential for forming lines of pieces. Encourages players to build longer lines.
18. *Line Cap*: Measures the player's potential to cap lines of enemy pieces at both ends. Encourages players to block enemy lines and increase the chance of linecap captures/conversions.
19. *Group*: Measures the player's potential for forming groups of specified size or content. Encourages players to gather pieces into connected groups.
20. *Connection*: Measures the potential to connect R target regions with a path of friendly pieces. Encourages players to strengthen the weakest point(s) in their strongest connection, as per good connective play.

Appendix D
List of Aesthetic Criteria

The following aesthetic criteria were implemented for Ludi's Criticism module. For further details of each including implementation notes see Browne [14]:

D.1 Intrinsic Criteria

Intrinsic criteria are those measured directly from the game's equipment and rules, without the need to play any games out. These include measurements of rule complexity, piece movement type and goal type.

1. *Complexity* is a measure of game's rule complexity, based on the number of items related to piece movement and winning conditions in its ludeme tree. Only piece movement and winning condition items are counted because these are the aspects with which players will be primarily concerned over the course of the game; rules relating to starting position and board configuration are taken for granted once the game has started.

Movement type indicates whether the game involves certain types of piece movement. This information is extracted directly from the game's *pieces* ludeme. The following movement types are detected:

2. *Addition,*
3. *Removal,*
4. *Movement,*
5. *Stacking,*
6. *Capture,*
7. *Conversion,* and
8. *Promotion.*

C. Browne, *Evolutionary Game Design*, SpringerBriefs in Computer Science, DOI: 10.1007/978-1-4471-2179-4, © Cameron Browne 2011

Goal type is a set features that indicate whether the game involves certain types of end conditions. This information is extracted directly from the game's *end* ludeme. The following goal types are detected:

9. *Connect,*
10. *Capture,*
11. *N-in-a-Row,*
12. *Race,*
13. *Group,*
14. *Stack,*
15. *Score,* and
16. *Block.*

D.2 Quality Criteria

Quality criteria are those measured during the course of play, typically from the game's lead histories. These attempt to capture trends in play that may indicate players' engagement over the course of the trials; these are the most difficult and least precise criteria to measure.

17. *Branching factor* (number of move choices per turn) indicates the combinatorial complexity of the game, and the amount of information that the player must process each turn to make reasonable moves. Branching factor may not be of overwhelming importance if the game has good clarity and it is easy to distinguish sound moves from unsound ones. For instance, Go is widely considered to be one of the very best combinatorial board games, despite having one of the largest branching factors at around 235 choices per move [17]. If a game has poor clarity, on the other hand, then too much complexity can appear as noise [32] and should be avoided if possible.
18. *Convergence* is the tendency for the number of moves available at each turn to decrease as the game progresses. Convergent games have the attractive property than an outcome is guaranteed after a certain number of moves. If branching factor is plotted against game duration, then convergence may be measured by the slope of this plot. A convergent game will slope downwards while a divergent game, in which the number of moves increases over the game's length, will slope upwards.
19. *Response time* measures the average amount of time required by computer player to formulate each move at its default settings. Like the branching factor criterion, this value indicates the amount of information the player must process each turn. However, response time also incorporates the complexity of the game's rules; games with larger branching factors and more complex rule sets will result in longer response times.

20. *Move effort* is the average number of lookahead moves visited in the computer's search for each move. Like the branching factor and response time criteria, this value indicates the amount of information the player must process each turn. It is somewhat more reliable than response time as its value will be independent of move complexity and the relative speeds of different advisor implementations.

21. *Search penetration* describes the average shape of the search tree created when formulating each move; a search is more penetrating if it is deep and narrow rather than shallow and wide. For each move of each game trial, the search ply of each node visited in the lookahead search leading up to that move is squared, accumulated then divided by the total number of search nodes.

22. *Clarity (variance)* measures the amount of variance in evaluations of the moves available to the current player at each turn. This is related to the concept of clarity as it models the amount of information the player must process to determine which moves are the most promising from the available choices. Special cases worth considering are games in which all moves are equally good, for instance those in which players take turns placing a piece on an empty cell and the winner is the first player unable to place a piece [3]. Despite having no outliers (all moves are equally good) such games will have maximum clarity and theoretically zero variance if the move estimates are accurate. The average variance in evaluations for each potential move is stored for each game trial, and the final result is the mean value over all trials.

23. *Clarity (narrowness)* measures the tendency for a small number of promising moves to stand out from the choices available at each turn. Like the variance measurement, this criterion is related to the game's clarity. Allis et al. [3] describe a pathological game played on a 19×19 Go board in which players take turns placing a piece of their colour, no capturing takes place, and the player to place the last piece wins. Such a game would have minimal narrowness as any move is as good as any other, and would also be of minimal interest to the players. For each move m_n, evaluations are made for all potential moves from the current board position. The average evaluation $E\square c(m_n)$ and maximum evaluation $Ecmax(m_n)$ are determined for this set of potential moves and the number falling at least 75% above the difference between the maximum and the mean are counted.

Uncertainty is the tendency for the outcome of the game to remain uncertain for as long as possible, ideally until a decisive lead is established in the last few moves. The sooner a game's outcome is known the less interesting it becomes (especially for the losing player). The amount of uncertainty is indicated by the area enclosed by the lead plot and an imaginary line from $(0, 0)$ to $(M, 1)$. This line describes a linear increase in lead over the course of the game, starting with a neutral lead of 0 and culminating with a winning lead of 1; this is the line of *average certainty* that a neutral game would be expected to follow. The game is uncertain if the majority of the enclosed area is below the line of average certainty and certain if the majority of the enclosed area is above this line. This area is approximated by taking $S = 100$ samples at regular intervals $t = [0..1]$ over the course of the game, and finding for each t the difference between the average certainty line and the interpolated value of the lead plot at this point. These differences are accumulated over all games and the average value for each t stored; the final result is the mean of these averages. The uncertainty criteria are divided into:

24. *Uncertainty (overall)*,
25. *Uncertainty (early)*, and
26. *Uncertainty (late)*.

Drama is the tendency for players to recover from seemingly bad positions. Drama is good for a game as it means that the leading player will not necessarily win the game and the eventual outcome remains uncertain until that lead becomes decisive. Drama is indicated by the number of moves that the eventual winner spends in a trailing position, and the severity of each such position. For each game, the *drama (average)* criterion gives the sum of these lead differences for each move divided by the total number of such moves. Drama is divided into:

27. *Drama (average)*, and
28. *Drama (maximum)*.
29. *Killer moves* estimates the tendency for *killer moves* to occur in a game. A killer move is one that significantly improves the player's position and typically swings the outcome of the game. Killer moves are therefore closely related to drama. Note that the term "killer move" has a different meaning here than in traditional game programming, where it refers to moves that help prune the game tree during adversarial search. Killer moves are measured by finding, for each game, the move that results in the greatest relative gain for the mover.
30. *Permanence* measures the tendency for players to immediately recover from the opponent's last move; games are described as *permanent* if the player cannot immediately recover to negate the effect of the opponent's last move. For each triplet of moves $\{m_{n-2}, m_{n-1}, m_n\}$, the decrease in relative board evaluation caused by the opponent's last move m_{n-1} is subtracted from the increase caused by the current player's replying move m_n. This is more meaningful than simply measuring the difference between the relative board evaluations at m_n and m_{n-2} as it incorporates the magnitudes of any decrease and subsequent correction.
31. *Lead change* indicates the tendency for the lead to change over the course of a game. This is indicated by the number of points at which the move history plots for both players cross each other, equivalent to the number of zero-crossings in the lead plot.
32. *Stability* is a measure of fluctuations in player's evaluations over the course of the game. This measure is closely related to the lead change and permanence measures. Games should generally have a moderate degree of stability; too

much stability can indicate a lack of drama, whereas too little stability can indicate a random game with little cohesion.

33. *Decisiveness threshold* indicates the point at which the leading player is generally known to have a winning advantage, that is, it can be stated that the leading player will go on to win the game with a reasonable degree of confidence. Ideally games should reach a conclusion quickly once this threshold is reached. The decisiveness threshold can be estimated by contradiction, by observing the maximum relative lead achieved by the loser over all histories for that game. In other words, it is the maximum lead that a player achieves without realising victory.

34. *Decisiveness* indicates whether a player wins quickly after reaching the decisiveness threshold for that game. Decisiveness is good as a game is of little interest once a player has established a commanding lead and is reasonably certain of victory. The decisiveness value is the ratio of moves after the decisiveness threshold is reached to the total number of moves, averaged over all game trials.

35. *Depth (discrepancy)* is a measure of the average difference between each move's shallow and deep evaluations. A move's *shallow evaluation* is the immediate board evaluation made after making the move (ply 1 lookahead) while a move's *deep evaluation* is result returned by a full alpha-beta search (ply N lookahead). Larger discrepancy values indicate that deeper (and theoretically more accurate) searches reveal information about a given board position that cannot be gleaned from immediate evaluations of the available moves. It can be argued that this hints at the depth of the game; experienced players with a deeper understanding of the game may prefer moves that novice players with a superficial understanding would overlook.

36. *Foulup factor* is the chance of a player making a serious mistake by overlooking a move. This is closely related to the clarity of a game, in addition to its obfuscation; this criterion measures the likelihood that the most obvious move is not the best one. For each move, the average ratio of alternative move choices with a better shallow evaluation than the actual move made is determined. This indicates the likelihood that a player will be deceived by immediate evaluations into choosing a suboptimal move. Suggested by Stephen Tavener.

Momentum is the tendency for the player in the lead to continue extending their lead with subsequent moves. Within each game trial, all triplets of moves $\{m_{n-2}, m_n, m_{n+2}\}$ are found such that $m_{n-2} < m_n$, and the momentum calculated as the ratio of such triplets in which $m_n < m_{n+2}$. In other words, momentum is the ratio of consecutive lead increases for either player that are followed by a subsequent lead increase on their next turn. The following momentum types are measures:

37. *Momentum*(1),
38. *Momentum*(2), and
39. *Momentum*(3).

Correction is the tendency for the lead to correct downwards following a consecutive lead increase by either player on their move. Correction is essentially the inverse of momentum; it describes the tendency for a game to normalise back towards a neutral position if either player starts to increase their lead. This category includes three related criteria: the correction calculation for lead increases over two consecutive moves m_{n-2} and m_n is called the *correction*(1) criterion; criterion *correction*(2) only performs this calculation for cases of lead increase over three consecutive moves m_{n-4}, m_{n-2} and m_n; and criterion *correction*(3) only performs this calculation for cases of lead increase over four consecutive moves m_{n-6}, m_{n-4}, m_{n-2} and m_n. Longer lead increases exist with increasing rarity. Correction is measured differently to momentum (by value rather than by count) so that these two measurements provide different interpretations of the base concept rather than just negated or inverted values of each other. There are three correction types:

40. *Correction*(1),
41. *Correction*(2), and
42. *Correction*(3).
43. *Control* measures the degree to which the leading player controls play by limiting the move choices of the opponent. This is not based on the number of legal moves (branching factor) but rather the number of positive moves available to the opponent. Control is generally seen as a positive quality that empowers the player [34], maintaining their interest in the game by allowing them to direct its course. Control also rewards forward thinking through tactical sequences of moves that force the opponent into traps. However too much control can be a bad thing, especially for the losing player, as it reduces the chance of a dramatic escape and means that the game is most likely headed for a predictable conclusion. This measurement utilises the narrowness calculation to estimate the number of obviously good moves available to the opponent. For each move m_n at which the current player has a significant (0.1) lead, the difference between the narrowness in replies available to the opponent and the mean narrowness for that game is measured.
44. *Coolness* is a measure of the degree to which players are forced to moves that harm their position. Cold situations are generally detrimental to a game as players seek to make the least-worst move rather than striving to make the most positive move each turn, which can be unsatisfying. Even worse, the game may degenerate into a *cold war* [13] in which players without positive move choices must make inconsequential moves until forced to make a decisive losing move. Such games are especially unsatisfying if the players can deduce long beforehand who will be forced to make the losing move. Coolness is measured as the average decrease in board evaluation for the current mover (if any) for each move.
45. *Board coverage* measures the ratio of the board cells visited by any piece over the course of each game. Low board coverage indicates that the game's starting position or movement rules may not be suitable for its board topology;

or perhaps the board is simply too big. The ratio of visited cells to total cells is stored for each trial, and the final value is the mean over all game trials.

46. *Puzzle quality* is an estimate of the difficulty of puzzles created for the game. In keeping with Sam Loyd's observation that his goal was to compose puzzles whose solutions require a first move that is contrary to what 999 players out of 1,000 would propose [26], a puzzle's quality is measured as the counter-intuitiveness of its solution (the winning move). This gives the number of winning lines available to the current mover—the eventual winner—at move m_n. If there is a single winning line for the current mover at m_n then this position constitutes a "win in three" puzzle with a unique solution. The puzzle quality is given by the number of moves with shallow evaluation better than the most highly valued winning line (this is a discrepancy measure for puzzles).

D.3 Viability Criteria

Viability criteria indicate whether the game is essentially viable, that is, whether it is playable without any obviously serious flaws, and would provide at least some degree of balanced contest between players. Viability criteria are typically based on discrete game outcomes, and are therefore easy to measure and robust. Several are similar to measurements described by Althöfer [4].

47. *Completion* is the tendency for games to reach a win or loss within a reasonable number of moves. Games that consistently fail to reach conclusive outcomes are generally unsatisfying. Completion is measured as the ratio of games that reach completion within the prescribed maximum number of moves.

48. *Balance* measures whether players of each colour have an equal chance of winning. Unbalanced games can obviously be unsatisfying for the disadvantaged player. Balance is measured as the absolute ratio of win difference between the two players, over all wins.

49. *Advantage* estimates any inherent *advantage* in a game, that is, the tendency for the first player (or sometimes the second) to win more than their fair share of games. Althöfer [4] describes this criterion as *balanced chances*. Advantage is measured as the absolute ratio of games that the first player wins above or below the expected 50% of games.

50. *Drawishness* is the tendency for a game to end in draws. This includes both ties (more than one winner) and draws (no winner). Technically draws should be included in the completion criterion as a draw constitutes a completed game, however it is worth keeping this information separate. Althöfer [4] describes this criterion as the *drawing quota*. Drawishness is given by the ratio of drawn games over all games.

51. *Timeouts* is a measure of the tendency for a game to fail to reach any sort of conclusive outcome (win, loss, draw) before the prescribed move limit is reached. An excessive number of timeouts indicate that a game may have serious flaws, such as goals that can never be reached.

52. *Duration* is a measure of the average number of moves required to complete a game. Although the length of each game in a set of trials will vary depending on the number of killer moves, miscalculations, dramatic recoveries and so on, ideally each game's duration should not deviate too far from the user's preferred number of moves, which is assumed to be half of the maximum specified game length. Game duration is useful for detecting pathological flaws in games in both direction; trivial games that end within a few moves, and excessively long games that are difficult to conclude. Game length is one of Althöfer's criteria [4]. Duration is measured as the average absolute deviation in the number of moves from the preferred number of moves per game, over all games.

53. *Depth(skill level)* indicates whether the game may be played at distinct skill levels [56]. It can be assumed that a stronger player will generally beat a weaker player. The likelihood of skill levels emerging may be indicated by observing whether a deeper-searching computer player generally outperforms an opponent making a shallower search, the analogy being that the player who searches deeper in the game tree has a deeper understanding of the game. The basic tenet of depth is that the more a player studies and understands a board position, the better the move they will make. This measurement is somewhat dubious as it is generally known that deeper search improves the strength of computer play, a phenomenon known as *deepening positivity* [4]. However, the degree of deepening positivity may yield some insights. Depth (skill level) is measured by reducing the search depth of one of the players by one ply; if this does not cause an appreciable difference then the game may be lacking in depth and of little interest.

54. *Selfishness* measures whether a player can get away with concentrating exclusively on their own piece development each turn. If such a player wins any games against a balanced opponent, this may point towards a lack of interaction in the game. Susceptibility to selfish play is measured by unbalancing one of the computer players to base their board evaluations exclusively on their own pieces; it is expected that this player should generally lose against a balanced opponent. The final value is the ratio of expected wins over all games.

55. *Obstructiveness* measures whether a player can get away with concentrating exclusively on their opponent's piece development each turn. If such a player wins any games against a balanced opponent, this may point towards a serious flaw in the game if a player can consistently win by impeding the opponent. This measure is less important for zero-sum games with mutually exclusive goals, such as Hex, in which a bad position for one player implies a good position for the opponent. Susceptibility to obstructive play is measured by unbalancing one of the computer players to base their board evaluations

exclusively on the opponent's pieces; it is expected that this player should generally lose against a balanced opponent. The final value is the ratio of expected wins over all games.

56. *Resilience* is the tendency for a game to withstand random moves from one of the players. If a random player wins *any* games against a balanced opponent, this may point to serious flaws either in the game or in the algorithm used to determine moves. For instance, random play would suit games that are so opaque that any move seems as good to any other, regardless of the player's skill. Susceptibility to random play means that players do not need to put much thought into each move and are therefore unlikely to engage intellectually with the game. This criterion measures the game's theoretical resilience to one of Borel's [10] dactylographic monkeys. Resilience to random play is measured by setting the search depth of one of the players to zero. It is expected that the zero depth player should always lose against a balanced opponent with search depth greater than 0. The final value is ratio of expected wins over all games.

57. *Puzzle potential* is an estimate of the ease with which puzzles may be created for the game. An inability to create puzzles may point to a flawed game [56]. "Win in three" puzzles are created using the same method as puzzle potential (both are measured at the same time). This criterion is one of the slowest to measure as it requires a separate run of trials with a full game tree expansion to depth 3 in each trial.

References

1. Abbott, R.: Under the strategy tree. Games & Puzzles 36 (1975)
2. Alden, S.: BoardGameGeek. http://www.boardgamegeek.com (2000)
3. Allis, L., Van den Herik, H., Herschberg, I.: Which games will survive? In: Levy, D., Beal, D. (eds.) Heuristic Programming in AI 2, pp. 232–243. Ellis Horwood, Chichester (1991)
4. Althöfer, I.: Computer-aided game inventing. Report, Friedrich Schiller Universitat, Jena (2003)
5. Back, T., Hoffmeister, F., Schwefel, H.: A survey of evolution strategies. In: Belew, R., Booker, L. (eds.) Genetic Algorithms, pp. 2–9. Morgan Kaufman, San Mateo (1991)
6. Baker, J.: Reducing bias and inefficiency in the selection algorithm. Proceedings of the Second International Conference on Genetic Algorithms and their Application, Lawrence Erlbaum Associates, Mahwah, pp. 14–21 (1987)
7. Berlekamp, E.R., Conway, J.H., Guy, R.K.: Winning ways for your mathematical plays, volumes 1: Games in general and 2: Games in particular. Academic Press, London (1982)
8. Birkhoff, G.D.: Aesthetic Measure. Harvard University Press, Cambridge (1933)
9. Boden, M.: The creative mind: myths and mechanisms. Routledge, London (1992)
10. Borel, E.: Mécanique Statistique et Irréversibilité. J. Phys. 5e série 3, pp. 189–196 (1913)
11. Borvo, A.: Anatomie d'un jeu de cartes: L'Aluette ou le Jeu de Vache, Librarie Nantaise Yves Vachon, Nantes, Paris (1977)
12. Browne, C.: Hex strategy: making the right connections. AK Peters, Massachusetts (2000)
13. Browne, C.: Connection games: variations on a theme. AK Peters, Massachusetts (2005)
14. Browne, C.: Automatic generation and evaluation of recombination games. PhD Thesis, QUT, Brisbane (2008)
15. Browne, C., Maire, F.: Evolutionary game design. IEEE Computational Intelligence & AI in Games. 2(1), 1–16 (2010)
16. Chaslot, G., Bakkes, S., Szita, I., Spronck, P.: Monte-Carlo tree search: a new framework for game AI. Proceedings of the Fourth Artificial Intelligence and Interactive Digital Entertainment Conference, AAAI Press, Menlo Park, pp. 216–217 (2008)
17. Coates, A.: Search space complexity. AI Depot, http://ai-depot.com/LogicGames/Go-Complexity.html (2005)
18. Costikyan, G.: Don't be a vidiot: what computer game designers can learn from non-electronic games. http://www.costik.com/vidiot.html (2005)
19. Dawkins, R.: The selfish gene. Oxford University Press, Oxford (1976)
20. Ellis, H.: Impressions and comments. Houghton Mifflin, Boston (1914)
21. Epstein, S.: Deep Forks in strategic maps: playing to win. In: Levy, D., Beal, D. (eds.) Heuristic programming in artificial intelligence 2: the Second Computer Olympiad, pp. 189–203, Ellis Horwood, Chichester (1991)

22. Eschelman, L., Schaffer, J.: Preventing premature convergence in genetic algorithms by preventing incest. Proceedings of the Fourth International Conference on Genetic Algorithms, pp. 115–122, Morgan Kaufmann, San Mateo (1991)
23. Gardner, M.: Theory of everything. The new criterion, **23**(2) (2004)
24. Genesereth, M., Love, N., Pell, B.: General game playing: overview of the AAAI competition. AI Magazine **26**(2), 62–72 (2005)
25. Greene, J.: Angband. http://members.cox.net/nppangband/download.htm (2007)
26. Hayward, R., Van Rijswijck, J.: Hex and combinatorics. Discret. Math. **306**, 2515–2528 (2006)
27. Holland, J.: Emergence: from Chaos to Order. Addison-Wesley, Redwood City (1998)
28. Horsten, L.: Philosophy of mathematics. http://plato.stanford.edu/entries/philosophy-mathematics (2007)
29. Iida, H., Takahara, K., Nagashima, J., Kajihara, Y., Hashimoto, T.: An application of gamerefinement theory to Mah Jong. ICEC 2004 (LNCS 3116), pp. 445–450. Springer, Berlin (2004)
30. Juillé, H., Pollack, J.B.: A stochastic search approach to grammar induction. ICGI'98, pp. 126–137. (1998)
31. Kernighan, B., Pike, R.: The practice of programming. Addison-Wesley, Reading (1999)
32. Koster, R.: A grammar of gameplay. http://www.theoryoffun.com/grammar/gdc2005.htm (2004)
33. Koza, J.: Genetic programming. MIT Press, Cambridge (1992)
34. Kramer, W.: What makes a game good? http://www.thegamesjournal.com (2000)
35. Langdon, W.: Data structures and genetic programming. In: Advances in Genetic Programming 2, pp. 395–414. MIT Press, Cambridge (1996)
36. Lovelace, A.: Notes on Menabrea's sketch of the analytical engine invented by Charles Babbage. In: Bowden, B.V. (ed.) Faster Than Thought. Pitman, London (1953)
37. Luke, S.: Essentials of metaheuristics. http://cs.gmu.edu/~sean/book/metaheuristics/ (2011)
38. Mallett, J., Lefler, M.: Zillions of games. http://www.zillions-of-games.com (1998)
39. Michalewicz, Z., Nazhiyath, G.: Genocop III. 2nd IEEE Conf on Evolutionary Computation, pp. 647–651. IEEE Press, Piscataway (1995)
40. Montana, D.: Strongly typed genetic programming. J. Evol. Comput. **3**, 199–230 (1995)
41. Nordin, P., Francone, F., Banzhaf, W.: Explicitly defined introns and destructive crossover in genetic programming. Report, University of Dortmund, (1995)
42. Parlett, D.: What is a ludeme? http://www.davidparlett.co.uk/gamester/ludemes.html (2007)
43. Pell, B.: Metagame in symmetric Chess-like games. In: Van den Kerik, H., Allis, L. (eds.) Heuristic Programming in Artificial Intelligence 3. Ellis Horwood, Chichester (1992)
44. Pell, B.: Strategy generation and evaluation for meta-game playing. Dissertation, University of Cambridge, Cambridge (1993)
45. Perlis, A.: Epigrams on programming. SIGPLAN Notices **17**(9), 7–13 (1982)
46. Pitrat, J.: Realisation of a general game-playing program. IFIP Congr **2**, 1570–1574 (1968)
47. Ritchie, G.: Some empirical criteria for attributing creativity to a computer program. Minds Machines **17**, 67–99 (2007)
48. Rolle, T.: Development of a multi-game engine. Dissertation, Friedrich-Schiller-Universitat, Jena (2003)
49. Romeral Andrés, N.: Nestorgames. http://www.nestorgames.com (2009)
50. Russell, S., Norvig, P.: Artificial intelligence: a modern approach, 2nd edn. Prentice Hall, New Jersey (2003)
51. Salen, K., Zimmerman, E.: Rules of play. MIT Press, Cambridge (2004)
52. Schmittberger, R.: New rules for classic games. John Wiley, New York (1992)
53. Soule, T., Foster, J.: Code size and depth flows in genetic programming. 2nd Conf on Genetic Programming, pp. 313–320. MIT Press, San Francisco (1997)
54. Stiny, G., Gips, J.: Algorithmic aesthetics. University Calif Press, Berkeley (1978)

55. Tackett, W.A.: Greedy recombination and genetic search on the space of computer Programs. In: Whiteley, D., Vode, M. (eds.) Foundations of Genetic Algorithms III. Morgan Kaufman, San Mateo (1995)
56. Thompson, M.: Defining the abstract. http://www.thegamesjournal.com (2000)
57. Wolfe, D.: The Gamesman's toolkit. In: Nowakowski, R. (ed.) Games of No Chance, pp. 93–98. Cambridge University Press, Cambridge (1996)

Index

A
Aesthetics
  aesthetic criteria, 24–36, 107–115
  aesthetic model, 25–26
  aesthetic measure, 24–25, 33–36
  algorithmic aesthetics, 24–25

C
Creativity
  computational, 2, 9
  computational, 2–3, 89–90
  H/P-creativity, 2, 72, 89
  in games, 3
  indicators, 2, 85, 89–90

E
Evolution
  bloat, 38, 48
  crossover, 40–41
  emergence, 38–39, 48, 57, 61, 67, 88
  genetic programming (GP), 38–39
  introns, 38–39, 45, 47–48, 73, 88
  mutation, 41–43, 48, 69, 88
  parent selection, 39
  parsimony pressure, 39–40, 46
  population, 38–39, 46–48, 88
  shortcomings, 60, 72–73, 88
  viability filter, 47–48, 58, 66, 88
Experiments
  game measurement, 33–36
  game ranking, 21
  game synthesis, 48–49

G
Game design
  computer aided, 37–38
  clarity, 24, 54, 56, 62, 108–109, 111
  decisiveness, 24, 28, 109–112
  depth, 24, 52, 54, 111, 114–115
  drama, 24, 29–31, 110–112
  first move advantage, 26, 28, 47, 59,
    79–82, 113
  kingmaker effect, 83
  quality, 3–4, 9, 24, 28–32, 108–113
  uncertainty, 24, 30, 47, 110
  viability, 26–28, 32–33, 47–48, 88,
    113–115
Games
  combinatorial, 6–7
  definition, 5–6
  Lammothm, 59–60, 73, 88
  game model, 5–6
  Ndengrod, 51–53, 72, 83, 87–89
  puzzles, 1–2, 6, 24, 36, 76–77, 113, 115
  recombination, 9, 40–41
  Tic Tac Toe, 7–10, 12–14, 20,
    40–41, 73
  variants, 8–10
  Yavalath, 1–2, 53–55, 72, 75–85, 87–90

L
Ludi
  baptism, 43
  criticism module, 11–12, 23, 26, 47
  game description language (GDL), 11–14,
    40, 91–104